ETHICS OF WORLD RELIGIONS

ETHICS OF WORLD RELIGIONS

(revised edition)

ARNOLD D. HUNT
MARIE T. CROTTY
ROBERT B. CROTTY

Greenhaven Press, Inc.
San Diego, California

Copyright © Robert Crotty 1976, 1991
First Published 1976 by Collins Dove
Revised edition published 1991 by Collins Dove
A division of HarperCollins*Publishers* (Australia) Pty Ltd.

ACKNOWLEDGEMENTS
The Bhagavad Gita translated by Juan Mascaro (Penguin Classics, 1962) copyright © Juan Mascaro, 1962.
Reproduced by permission of Penguin Books Ltd.

The Dhammapada translated by Juan Mascaro (Penguin Classics, 1973), copyright © Juan Mascaro, 1973.
Reproduced by permission of Penguin Books Ltd.

Our thanks go to those who have given us permission to reproduce material in this book.

Library of Congress Cataloging-in-Publication Data

Hunt, A. D. (Arnold Dudley)
    [Set your heart on goodness]
    Ethics of world religions/Arnold D. Hunt, Robert B. Crotty, Marie T. Crotty.
        p. cm.
    Previously published in Australia as: Set your heart on goodness.
    Includes bibliographical references and index.
    Summary: Compares and contrasts the ethical systems derived from the major religions of the world.
    ISBN 0-89908-824-4 (lib. bdg.) ISBN 0-89908-823-6 (pbk.)
    1. Religious ethics. [1. Religious ethics. 2. Social values.]
    I. Crotty, Robert, C.P. II. Crotty, Marie T. III. Title.
    BJ1188.H86 1991
    291.5—dc20   91-21259

© Copyright 1991 by Greenhaven Press, Inc.

Contents

Authors	1
Preface	3
Introduction	4
Judaism	13
Christianity	45
Islam	83
Hinduism	109
Buddhism	131
Confucianism	157
Australian Aboriginal religions	181
Conclusion	195
Recommended reading	203
Glossary	207
Index	211

Major world religions

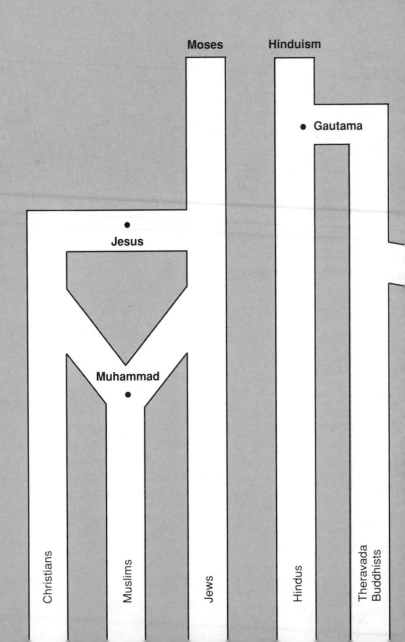

Moses

Hinduism

• Gautama

•
Jesus

Muhammad
•

Christians

Muslims

Jews

Hindus

Theravada
Buddhists

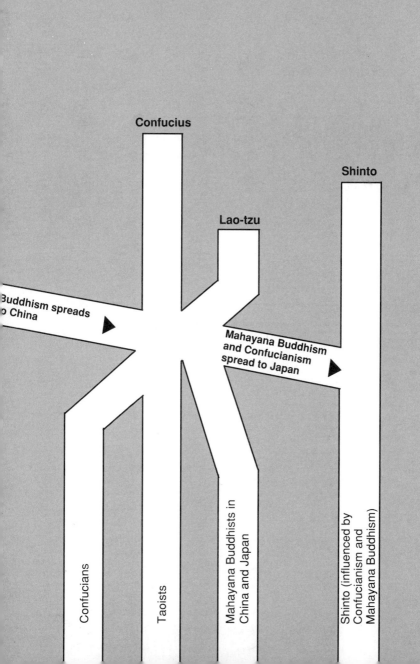

Authors

Arnold D. Hunt BA (Adelaide), BD Hons (Melbourne College of Divinity), PhD (Hartford).

Formerly Principal Lecturer and Head of the Department of History and Religion Studies, South Australian College of Advanced Education, Salisbury. Earlier Arnold had been Principal of Parkin-Wesley Theological College. He trained for the Methodist ministry and then spent six years in India as a missionary. Now retired, he continues, amongst other activities, to write and lecture on Asian religions.

Robert B. Crotty STL (Rome), SSL (Rome), MA (Melbourne), PhD (Adelaide), Élève Titulaire de l'École Biblique (Jerusalem).

Senior Lecturer and Head of the Department of History and Religion Studies, University of South Australia. Robert studied theology and biblical studies in Australia, Rome and Jerusalem. He has lectured in various theological colleges and written widely on religions of the Middle East.

Marie T. Crotty BA (Monash), MEd (Adelaide), DipT, GradDipT.

Sociologist and Lecturer in the School of Library and Information Management, University of South Australia. Marie has done research in the fields of women's studies and curriculum, particularly as regards religious education.

Preface

A new edition of *Ethics of World Religions* has given us the opportunity to revise the text. Although the original had a wide reception and kind reviews and was used in a variety of teaching situations, it was clear that some changes had to be made.

The perennial problem that besets authors in this field is that of nomenclature. How are 'ethics' and 'morals' to be differentiated? For the sake of clarity we follow modern theorists who use 'morals' to refer to the actual human behaviours while 'ethics' refers to the formal argumentative structure which justifies that moral behaviour. This is explained in more detail in the text.

Since the first edition, language usage has changed. Every effort has been made to ensure that the book's language treats males and females equally. In certain cases the patriarchal framework of past societies has had to be accepted and 'men' is used where males were specifically intended. Also, some texts in translation contain sexist references simply because the original texts were sexist in their usage.

Instead of BC we use BCE (Before the Common Era) and CE (Common Era) instead of AD.

During the past fifteen years, significant new moral problems have been raised and new ethical arguments proposed. The revised text tries to address these and place the new perspectives within the context of the various world religions.

Introduction

What are ethics and morals?

What do we mean when we talk about 'ethics' and 'morals'? Morals is a description of actual human behaviour. When we discuss the fact that some people steal, that some people care for the sick and elderly, we are talking about morals. Ethics describes the justification for, the argument and reasoning behind, such human behaviour. If we were to talk about why people should care for the sick and elderly, or why people should not steal, then we would be talking about ethics. You will notice that we often use the language of ethics and morals. When we say 'People ought to do this or that', or 'This or that is wrong', we are using the language of ethics and morals.

Sometimes we use these terms in a nonchalant way. We can say, for instance, 'People ought to clean their shoes before leaving the house'. But when we say, 'You ought not kill!' we express a principle which everyone would recognise as a serious attempt to regulate behaviour.

Two characteristics distinguish moral statements. First, moral statements are directed towards people as free beings. 'You ought not kill' has no moral meaning if directed to the non-human—the shark or the tractor. It has no moral meaning if spoken to someone who is not fully responsible—the psychopath or the baby. It only has moral meaning when spoken to the person who is faced with the decision to kill or not to kill and who can freely choose one way or another.

Second, moral statements are directed to free persons in matters which affect individuals or society in a significant way.

We should now be able to say how ethics affects human behaviour. There are certain goals, significant in themselves, which are considered worthy of attainment by at least some people. Ethical arguments and ethical reasoning indicate that some free, human actions are good or bad in relation to such a goal. Finally, certain attitudes or values motivate people to pursue these goals, accept the ethical arguments and behave accordingly. A goal could be peaceable co-existence in society. An ethical argument might maintain that in order to achieve this goal the Bible (or a great philosopher or human logic) forbids wanton murder. The attitude or value that would bring people to accept such behaviour would be respect for human life.

Ethical variety

People have been, and still are, guided by ethical systems. These ethical systems can be said to justify free, human behaviour in significant areas. To act according to such ethical reasoning would be, the proponents of the systems claim, to act in a genuinely human fashion. People have often sought an answer to the question 'What does it mean to be human?' The Greek writer Heraclitus insisted that the meaning of the world could not be unfolded until the human mystery was first solved. Socrates called for self-scrutiny—'Know thyself!' he advised, 'An unexamined life is not worth living!'

What does it mean to be human? There have been many answers to the question. During our own lifetime, we may answer that question in different ways. It is not simply a talking point for philosophers; it is a question that can cause anguish and concern, and lead on to other questions: Who am I? What shall I become? How can I realise my fullness? What can be done about the discord and incompleteness of human life? People try to understand themselves in order to become fully themselves and give shape and direction to their lives. The moral practice of any person is founded on the answers supplied to these questions.

Answers can be discovered in many ways, imposed from outside, borrowed from others or arrived at by personal effort and perseverance. Some people become uncomfortable with imposed or borrowed answers; they want to see other possibilities. Others are content to accept and borrow answers which give them security.

From the variety of answers to the question of a person's direction in life arise many ethical systems. Some of these ethical systems are religious.

Religious ethics

This book presents some of the ethical systems of the world religions. They do differ. They do provide various answers to the question: 'What does it mean to be human?' That variety can only be appreciated when it is realised that there are various ways to be human. Even though we humans all belong to one genus, *Homo sapiens*, there can be significant differences between one group and another. Why?

We human beings are strange creatures. Like other animals we need food, drink and shelter and like them we need to have order in our everyday life. A horse, for example, has a certain order in its day-to-day life. It eats only certain food, does not drink certain fluids, sleeps in a certain way at certain times, mates almost according to a programme, and cares for its young according to a pattern. By instinct the horse knows what to do, when to do it, how to do it. It has order. We are different, in so far as we are not born with so many instinctual instructions. We have to learn a way of life, to acquire a common set of understandings whereby we, together with like-minded people, can find a satisfactory and fairly peaceable lifestyle. That way of life is what anthropologists call our culture. Culture is more than art and music. It is a patterned way of thinking and acting. It is learned and then tenaciously handed on from one generation to the next, and it can differ considerably from one group of humans to another. A Chinese culture, its common set of understandings, is quite different from Anglo Saxon culture. Nowadays, in a multicultural society, we say that neither culture is 'true' or 'better'. They both work.

But human difference does not stop with having to learn how to behave instead of knowing at birth, like the horse. We want more than just sufficient order to get through one day at a time. We ask deeper questions than the horse: Is life worth living? Who am I, after all? Where is life taking me? What is going to happen beyond death? Why do some innocent people, like little children, suffer and even die? Everyday culture does not provide an answer to such ultimate questions. Human beings need another system, another way of life, another set of common understandings. These are the 'religions' of the world. Not only the conventional religions (such as Christianity or Hinduism) are included but the 'isms' (Marxism, Humanism) and hybrid, personal systems. We have no common term to cover them.

How do these religions make an impact on human beings? Each presents itself as a pattern of symbols: stories, activities, artifacts, statements of belief, buildings, and so on. The symbols are woven together to present a coherent 'world' where religious adherents feel at home.

How are we to distinguish between one religious 'world' and another? Are all religions really the same? Is one religion correct? There are at least three attitudes that are possible.

1. One religion is the correct one and all others are false. This is called 'exclusivism', because it *excludes* all religions except the one to which 'I' belong.
2. One religion is the correct one, but many other religions do have real value. Some Christians, for example, would say that while Christianity is the one true religion, God is at work in other religions. Non-Christians are as good as Christians. During the Second Vatican Council many Catholics took up this position which is often called 'inclusivism'.
3. All religions are correct and true. Just as we have many cultures—European, Chinese, Arab—so we have many religions. Cultures are all 'true' for the people who follow them; so too are religions. Each one achieves its purpose of bringing ultimate order into people's lives. There may be real differences between religions, but they do not affect the goal of each one, the quest for ultimate reality. This is called 'pluralism'.

This book does not presuppose any one of the three attitudes. In a society that is multicultural, shared by many peoples from different ethnic backgrounds, it is the third approach that is often encouraged. However, there are many people who espouse the other two attitudes.

Each religious culture has its own particular order. Each one proposes how our human behaviour should be regulated. How am I to know whether I should eat with my hands or with knife and fork? My everyday culture instructs me. It also regulates behaviour that affects individuals or society in more significant ways. It regulates morality and provides moral directives. Religious culture also instructs me. It also formulates moral statements concerning human behaviour and devises an ethical system to justify that moral behaviour. Those moral statements and those ethical systems that derive from religious cultures are the focus of this book.

Justifying human behaviour

How do particular religious groups justify their decisions about behaviour that is permitted or forbidden or prescribed? How does a religious group know whether its married members can divorce, whether they can engage in war, whether they can take another's personal belongings? There are a variety of sources from which such justification is obtained.

First, there are sacred stories. One of Judaism's creation stories about Adam and Eve tells of a rib being taken from Adam's side and fashioned into a woman, Eve. Eve is then brought to Adam who recognises her as a very part of himself. Adam then says: 'This is now bone of my bone and flesh of my flesh'. The Hebrew text implies that the woman will co-operate with him in good times (bone) and support him in adversity (flesh). The story concludes that this is why men and women unite sexually in marriage and they become one body or person. The story justifies sexuality in marriage.

Linked to sacred stories are the second source, sacred texts. Written texts, accepted as divinely guided writings, may prescribe a behaviour or forbid a behaviour. 'Love one another as I have loved you', says Jesus in the New Testament, and the commandment of love of the other has become an unassailable feature of Christian morality.

A third source is the sacred ritual practised by a particular religious group. It can indicate a dramatic turning-point affecting behaviour. A Buddhist is ordained as a monk and immediately thereafter is liable to 227 rules. A Christian is married in a Christian ritual and may have sexual relations with the partner, whereas such behaviour is forbidden to the non-married.

Religions are socially constructed with a hierarchy of authority and power. This social structure constitutes a fourth source of justification. In some religions women are regarded as inferior and so it is expected that they will obey men and be submissive to them. A particular person may be elevated to a superior social status in the religion, as a tribal elder or a Pope. Such persons, on their own authority, may be able to declare what is forbidden or permitted.

Religious experience is a fifth source. A religious founder may have had a profound religious experience in which a moral requirement has been communicated. The founder may have been told to avoid eating a type of food. Such a mandate stands. Or perhaps a religious devotee cannot decide whether a behaviour is forbidden or permitted. In prayer, an 'answer' is received and the person is assured of the proper moral stance.

Finally, there is justification from religious belief. All religions give rise to beliefs: beliefs about that which is beyond this world, gods and divine beings or states of being; beliefs about the way the world has been established and is structured; beliefs about how humans can be saved. Such beliefs justify human behaviours. Because Theravadin Buddhists believe that by mental concentration they can attain Nirvana, they are forbidden intoxicants which would hinder such an attainment.

We have seen that morality in human behaviour can be justified by ethical reasoning. That ethical reasoning takes its rise from the basic question: 'What does it mean to be human?' Perhaps a particular religion sees 'being human' as something less important, even something unreal. Or a religion may see 'being human' as very important, full of possibility. Different religions will devise different ethical systems, different ethical reasonings, as they answer that question: 'What does it mean to be human?'

About this book

There is value in reviewing the ethical systems of the world religions. Perhaps one of them will offer a fulfilling way of life. Perhaps all of them will be rejected and the search continued.

The chapters that follow will not simply list 'rights' and 'wrongs' in the world religions. The shape of each ethical system will be presented, and the way of life that it offers. The ethical system will be seen in the context of the entire religion.

This book does not offer any judgements, it describes; it does not evaluate or compare. People have the opportunity to shape their own life according to their own account of what it means to be human.

1
Judaism

The menorah or 'seven-branched candlestick' once stood in the Temple of Jerusalem. It was removed by the Romans when they destroyed the Temple in 70 CE. It has become the symbol of Judaism, and its significance is variously described as the unquenchable spirit of Judaism, the light of God, the tree of life.

Main dates of Judaism

Patriarchal clans in Canaan	▼	1800
Hebrews in Egypt		1500
Exodus from Egypt	*c.*	1300
Israel conquers Canaan		1200
David elected king		1000
Schism divides Kingdom of Solomon		922
Assyrians defeat Northern Israel		722
Code of Deuteronomy		622
Jerusalem destroyed by Babylon		587
Priestly tradition predominant	▼	
Return from exile		538
Greeks conquer the land of Israel		331
Rome conquers the land of Israel		63
		CE
Temple destroyed and dispersion of Jews	▼	70
Completion of Talmud	▼	500
Jewish philosophy flourishes	▼	1000
Persecution of Jews in Europe begins	▼	1200
Emigration of European and Russian Jews, especially to USA	▼	1800
Return of Jews to Palestine	▼	1882
Zionist movement founded		1897
Nazi persecution of Jews		1933
Establishment of State of Israel		1948

You shall not seek revenge or sustain anger towards your own people; you shall love your neighbour as a person like yourself. I am Yahweh.

Judaism

On the evidence of those Jewish texts that have come down to us, it seems that the people of ancient Israel rarely discussed philosophical issues about good and evil; they seemed to have produced prophets rather than moral philosophers. Their ethical system was mainly fashioned by their religious experience, lived out in day-to-day existence. For Israel, what was good and desirable was what their god, Yahweh, demanded: evil was what Yahweh forbade. To understand such a statement, more must be learnt about both ancient Israel and the god Yahweh.

Key

Early Israel

According to the biblical narrative, the history of Israel began with the call of the patriarch Abraham. He was invited to undertake a journey, leaving behind his family heritage, and to seek a new life in the land of Canaan. He accepted the invitation and eventually settled in that land. He was succeeded as patriarch of the group by his son, Isaac, who, in his turn, was succeeded by a son Jacob, also known as Israel. Jacob-Israel had twelve sons by four wives. When famine descended on the land the whole tribal group left Canaan and settled in Egypt. At first they were welcomed. Later they were seen as a threat to the Egyptians, and a programme of genocide began. Under the shadow of annihilation one Israelite, Moses, assumed leadership. He led the people out of Egypt, guided and protected by a new god—Yahweh. The journey out of Egypt was called the Exodus, and it was accompanied by great wonders. At a mountain known as either Sinai or Horeb, the Israelites and Yahweh made a covenant, a treaty. Yahweh promised to be their god, to guide them and give them victory if they obeyed him. They promised to be his people. And so the group returned to the land of Canaan from which their ancestors had departed. Under Joshua, the successor of Moses, they defeated the inhabitants of the land and took possession of it.

That was Israel's story. It explained their origins and their direction in life. The story was also the basis for their ethics. Historians, however, would want to express the story in a somewhat different way. They would say, for example, that during the period from 3000 BCE there were waves of Semitic migration pouring into the arc of land bounded by Mesopotamia, Canaan and Egypt. The arc has become known as the Fertile Crescent, since it has sufficient rainfall and vegetation to allow semi-nomadic people to wander with sheep and goats. Due to increased population in the Arabian peninsula there were periodic migrations into the Crescent. Archaeology has demonstrated that one such wave of people arrived between 2100 BCE and 1700 BCE. These people formed a series of city-states in the western area and there they developed a sophisticated culture. They were the Canaanites. Another wave arrived between 1400 BCE and 900 BCE. Somewhere amid this movement of peoples, during the second millenium BCE, there could well have been a group of Semites led by a patriarch Abraham. Apart from the biblical story there is, however, no direct evidence of him. There would also, presumably, have been groups led by an Isaac and a Jacob. These three would not have necessarily been related. Upon arrival they settled in Canaan and began to adapt their religious practice to the new situation they found there.

Before their migration to the west these groups practised

a clan religion, each clan protected by its own god, chosen by a leader. The clan god was the one who knew the routes that the nomads must take and who protected the whole group and its livestock from ever present dangers. Worship was very simple, with no regular priesthood. The main ritual was animal sacrifice to implore the protection and blessing of the clan god. During the period when clans settled in the land of Canaan, they would have adapted their simple clan religion to the already established religion of the Canaanites. They were no longer wandering nomads; they were becoming agriculturalists.

The Canaanites' religion included a whole pantheon of gods. The main god, although for practical purposes not the most important, was 'El. 'El had a son Ba'al, the god of the storm and of fertility. According to their myth, the sacred story of the Canaanites, Ba'al had a consort 'Anath. In battle he was defeated by another god, Mot, and during the period of his eclipse the whole of nature languished. There were no crops; neither women nor animals gave birth. When he returned all nature revived.

Most Canaanite worship focussed on Ba'al. People recited his sacred story and implored his help. Earlier, worship had been offered to 'El and, particularly in the outlying areas, this worship persisted. The Semitic clans came into contact with the worship of 'El and identified their clan gods with him. They performed the acts of ritual practised by the Canaanites in honour of their own clan gods.

Most historians would say that the third and vital stage in the transformation of the Semitic groups was connected with Egypt. There is a good deal of evidence to show that Semitic peoples lived in Egypt. Sometimes the Egyptians took them there as prisoners; sometimes famine in the Fertile Crescent drove them there. They were sometimes forced into compulsory labour by the Egyptian rulers. We can conjecture, historically, that something like the following events took place. One Semitic group was at first welcomed into Egypt and allowed to live in comparative peace. This would have coincided with an unusual period in Egyptian history when Semitic people had actually seized the throne. Later the rule reverted to native Egyptians who naturally feared that Semites living within their borders could assist in a new uprising. So the Semitic group was threatened with extinction.

Exodus and covenant

They were saved by a leader called Moses. He married a foreign woman, a Midianite, from a people living a semi-nomadic way of life in the south of Canaan and on the very borders of Egypt. Moses' father-in-law, Jethro, was a priest of this people. The Midianites may well have worshipped a god called Yahweh, who was very much like the god 'El, but went by a different name. Moses, through Jethro, came to know and appreciate the power of Yahweh. Eventually he went back to his people in Egypt and announced that this Yahweh would give them victory and allow them to escape from their oppression.

In some way the group did escape from Egypt, and they attributed this escape to Yahweh. Arriving in Canaan they found the earlier clans forming a tribal system. The newly-arrived immigrants offered to the tribes the worship and the protection of the new god, Yahweh. Yahweh proved his worth by giving victory in battle and one by one the tribes were converted. Eventually the immigrant group was completely absorbed into twelve tribes, all of whom became worshippers of Yahweh. 'Israel' came into being at that time, as a confederation of tribes.

The people of Israel discovered that they were united not by blood or a shared history but by a common faith in the god Yahweh. The various peoples who made up Israel then pooled their traditions. Some looked back to a patriarchal figure, Abraham, others to Isaac, others to Jacob.

Others were descended from the immigrant group led by Moses. All traditions regarding settlement in Canaan, escape from Egypt, and subsequent victory in battle became common property. That was the beginning of the sacred story of Israel. As far as the Israelites were concerned, Yahweh had been guiding and directing their destiny from the beginning. The clan gods of the nomads, who had been earlier identified with 'El, were now identified with Yahweh. This story is not history as we would write history today, but that is not the important point. The story does explain the life of the people of Israel—who they were and where they were going. It is the sacred story that is important in order to understand Israel and Israel's ethical system, not its history.

No matter what the actual sequence of events was, it is essential to grasp the fact that Israel believed that it was created by a personal encounter with Yahweh. He had entered Israel's life in the Exodus from Egypt and that crucial event, as told in its story, became the basis for all later belief and expectation. Later generations of Israelites believed that just as Yahweh had directed and guided Moses, so he directed and guided them. They sought to know his will for they were convinced that he would be true to them as he had been to Moses and his followers. This confidence was based on the covenant Yahweh had made with Moses.

A covenant is a treaty, an agreement between partners. Amongst the people who surrounded the early Israelites, covenants were widely used to maintain peace and stability in both domestic and international dealings. When Israel wanted to express the fact that Yahweh had intervened in its history, it said that he had made a covenant. The covenant was made solely on the initiative of Yahweh and imposed obligations on the people of Israel. Those obligations were the very essence of its morality. By understanding the covenant relationship one comes to an understanding of moral practice in Israel.

Yahweh's actions towards Israel and Israel's response towards him make up the covenant. Israel's covenant was always patterned on the first relationship that took place between Moses' group and Yahweh. Similarly the response of the first group was seen as the pattern for all other groups who responded. It is that first response then, seen through the eyes of later Israel, that laid the basis of its ethical system.

Yahweh, taking the side of Israel, showed what Israel called *hesed*, 'covenant love', the undeserved care and concern of Yahweh for this people. It was accompanied by an unswerving love which Israel called *'emeth* or 'truth'. The response of Israel to this *hesed* and *'emeth* of Yahweh is called *'emunah* or 'faithfulness'. *'Emunah* is the constant fulfilment of the obligations that Yahweh's activity demands. When people lived by *'emunah* they were righteous; the relationship between themselves and Yahweh was fit and proper. The righteous Israelite read Yahweh's activity correctly and learnt how to respond faithfully to it. A prophet could write,

'The righteous person will find life by means of *'emunah.*'

Habakkuk 2: 4

The Way and the law

Israel described the moral demands of the covenant that Yahweh laid down as the *derek* or 'Way'. The Israelite who was faithful 'walked in the Way' or 'went in the Way'. There was a beginning to this Way and a final end and there was a right intention that led the Israelite along the Way. Yahweh, according to this metaphor, was the leader, the guide or the shepherd. The very essence of sinfulness was for people to walk their own way on the basis of their own self-sufficiency. True morality and the ethics of Israel demanded that they perceive the activity of Yahweh in the world and respond to that activity.

The Way of Israel was also known as the Torah or law, but Israel's Torah does not correspond to the Western ideas of law. The Torah comprises the first five books of the Bible in which the God of Israel manifested himself to his people and called them to respond to him. The books were called the Torah because in this revelation the people of Israel saw what Yahweh required, what was the good, what they should do. The Israelites' attitude towards the Torah can be seen in some of the Psalms where pious poets speak of their love for it:

> How happy are they who are blameless in the Way
> Who walk in the Torah of Yahweh.
> How happy are they who respect his decrees
> Who seek him with all their heart.
> Indeed they do no evil
> And they walk in his ways.
>
> Psalm 119*

There is no arid legalism here, but a love and a desire to respond to Yahweh.

Prophets—Israel's conscience

The prophets of Israel were the ones who perceived Yahweh's activity most clearly and who gave voice to his demands. They called Israel to make a decision. They made the Way ever more explicit for their fellow Israelites. Prophets were not foretellers of the future. They were interpreters of the present, whose gift was the ability to read the present moment and its meaning.

The prophets condemned self-sufficiency. They condemned kings who were not totally subservient to Yahweh, kings who sought their security in foreign treaties and not in the Torah. They denounced them with contempt.

* All biblical quotations in this chapter have been translated from the Hebrew by the author.

Woe to those who go down to Egypt for help
who place their trust in horses
relying on chariots,
or in horsemen because they are strong.
They do not look to the Holy One of Israel,
nor do they seek Yahweh!

Isaiah 31: 1

Kings, priests, fellow prophets, common people who did not act in accordance with the Torah of Yahweh were reprimanded in this way. In Israel there was no place for self-sufficiency. Trust in Yahweh was the pre-requisite for accepting the ethical system of Israel.

By the ninth century BCE the semi-nomadic life that the tribes had once known was gone. Only the memory remained. Mercantilism had spread from the more settled north and there was dishonesty, exploitation of the poor and a growing disparity between the haves and the have-nots. Some Israelites lived in luxury while their compatriots lived in need. The prophets insisted that the covenant meant the equality of all Israelites. Yahweh had equal concern for all individuals in Israel. They gave vent to their anger:

Therefore, since you have trodden underfoot the poor
and taken their wheat from them,
you will not dwell in the houses you built of hewn stone,
nor drink wine from the luxuriant vineyards you have planted.

Amos 5: 11

One theme often recurred—the land would punish the transgressor. The land had been promised to all Israelites by Yahweh, who remained its owner.

The Land is not to be sold in perpetuity. The Land is mine!
You are strangers and travellers with me.

Leviticus 25: 23

For the Canaanites it had been Ba'al who bestowed fertility on the land. For the Israelites it was Yahweh who made the land fertile, not in response to a ritual properly performed, but in response to the proper fulfilment of the Torah. Lack of moral response could only bring ruin upon the land and upon Israel.

Since the community of Israel had to resolve its own conflicts according to the Torah of Yahweh, the prophets insisted on the correct administration of justice. There was no place for privilege or discrimination when the elders met at the town gates to decide what was right and wrong. Judges were merely the mouthpiece of Yahweh. Taking bribes and depriving the righteous of their legal due were abominable practices within Israel.

> Woe to those who make the wicked righteous for a bribe and who take away the righteousness of the righteous.
>
> Isaiah 5: 23

The prophetic writings show that the ethical reasoning of Israel developed from her history. Yahweh had chosen this people to be his very own. He showed them *hesed* and *'emeth* and demanded that they respond to him with *'emunah*. They were to become righteous by following the Way that Yahweh had shown, by keeping his Torah. The Way or the Torah of Israel included, in the first place, the maintenance of the special relationship that bound the people to Yahweh. In the second place, the Torah demanded that a proper relationship be maintained between person and person in the covenant group. The prophets simply made plain and clear what was called for in practice. They were the conscience of Israel.

Laws and codes

In Exodus, chapters 21–3, there is the so-called Covenant Code. As part of Israel's story it is the outline of the law, the Way to Yahweh, given to Moses on Sinai. It was probably the earliest code of laws that Israel produced, built up over the period of the twelve-tribe confederation.

It would have reached a permanent form before the time of the monarchy in the tenth century BCE. Doubtless some of the material was borrowed from neighbouring cultures, particularly laws that maintained order and stability in society. Other ancient law codes, particularly those from Mesopotamia, are principally concerned with property rights and the protection of the powerful; but the laws of Israel protected the entire community and were motivated by Israel's own religious spirit. Israel firmly asserted that the authority of her laws derived from Yahweh.

The Covenant Code began with a statement on the worship of Israel. There were to be no idols, whether of Yahweh or of any other god. In this way Israel stated her conviction that Yahweh could not be manipulated in any way by his people. Access to the image of gods meant, to ancient peoples, the ability to control those gods, to require their presence and demand their action. This was not the relationship between Yahweh and Israel.

The Code then stipulated that slaves within Israel were to be freed after a certain period of service, and this law was followed by the law of retaliation:

Life in return for life
eye in return for eye
tooth in return for tooth
hand in return for hand
foot in return for foot
burning in return for burning
wounding in return for wounding
maiming in return for maiming.

Exodus 21: 23–5

In tribal societies, justice was enforced by a law which limited revenge. When someone was wronged, the law of retaliation allowed retribution to be taken only to the extent that injury had been inflicted. It was a progressive law, not a law of uncivilised society.

The final section of the Covenant Code consisted of

religious laws concerning, first of all, the Sabbatical Year. In every seventh year, Israelites were commanded to allow their land to lie fallow. Just as humans and even animals were granted rest every seven days, so the land was to be rested every seventh year. This seems to be, of course, very impractical. Food would have to be stored up for that seventh year. Perhaps it was more an ideal rather than a binding obligation. The great feasts to be celebrated by all Israelites were also named: the Feast of Unleavened Bread (Pesach), the Feast of Weeks (Shavuot) and the Feast of Tents (Sukkot). All of these celebrated aspects of the Exodus from Egypt.

The Covenant Code shows the special response demanded by Yahweh from his own people. They were to form a particular type of community in which there were to be no class distinctions, apart from the fact that the institution of slavery was accepted. The laws bound all Israelites equally since all of Israel had once undergone the Exodus out of Egypt. All had experienced the *hesed* of Yahweh and all must respond. So the code expressed concern for the oppressed, and demanded care for the disinherited, the weak, the poor and the afflicted. Since Yahweh had brought his people from the oppression of Egypt to freedom and a new life, no one in Israel was unimportant.

The Code of Deuteronomy, found in Deuteronomy 5–26, is a later expansion of the Covenant Code. In Israel's story Moses farewelled his people with a series of sermons as they were about to take possession of the land. This Code was set down centuries after the Covenant Code when the new institutions of monarchy and statehood were well advanced. Its aim was, in general, to restore the vibrant faith of Moses' time to a people who were culturally different from the first confederation of tribes. Laws were expanded to include the new institutions and the king of Israel was specifically mentioned. But the motivation remained the same. Yahweh's *hesed*, first experienced by Israel in the Exodus and then in all the later events of Israel's life, must be reciprocated with obedience. This obedience meant, in the first place, adhering faithfully to Yahweh and, secondly, maintaining the covenant community of Israel.

The Ten Commandments

Traditionally, the Ten Commandments have been the principal expression of the moral stance of Israel. They are found in the books of both Exodus (20: 2–17) and Deuteronomy (5: 6–21). Series of commandments or prohibitions are well known among nomadic and semi-nomadic peoples in the ancient Middle East. Often they occur in groups of ten. These commandments are not so much hard and fast laws as general rules of conduct, indicating the kind and quality of life that should be found in the group. The story of Israel claimed that Yahweh handed down the Ten Commandments on Sinai. Historians would debate about the dating of their final written form, but they seem to be a summing up of several earlier series of rules.

The most basic moral demand of the Ten Commandments was to worship Yahweh alone. This was in line with the prohibition of self-sufficiency and self-determination. Yahweh was the sole god of Israel, a god of freedom who acted when he so willed and chose Israel to be his people, not because of their greatness or goodness but, paradoxically, because of their weakness and need. Some of the other rules of conduct in the Ten Commandments must have gone back to Israel's earliest days—laws that regulated the life of a nomadic group and ensured its stability. We will consider these rules of conduct in some detail.

As they stand in the biblical text of Exodus 20: 1–17 and Deuteronomy 5: 6–21 the Ten Commandments are headed by a brief summary of Israel's story:

> I myself am Yahweh your God who brought you out from the land of Egypt, from the house of slavery.

The first commandment stated the absolute demand that Yahweh should alone be the God of Israel. There was to be no recourse to other gods, no petitioning of them (even if Israel believed them to be real), no access to their worship:

There shall be no other gods among you in worship!

The second commandment also referred to Yahweh:

You shall not fashion any image nor any likeness of anything in the heaven above, or on the land below or in the sea or under the earth!

The power of Yahweh could not be manipulated. Other gods might have their power focussed into an idol of an animal, a fish, an astral body, but not Yahweh. Later, this commandment was expanded to forbid the use of the idols of other gods:

You shall not bow down in worship before them or serve them, for I am Yahweh your God, a God of Jealousy, who inflicts punishment for the sinfulness of parents who hate me on children to the third and fourth generation. But I offer my *hesed* to the thousandth generation to those who love me and keep my commandments.

The third commandment forbade the use of Yahweh's name in magical incantations or in any ritual which might seek to control him:

You shall not misuse the name of Yahweh your God, for Yahweh will not leave the person unpunished who misuses his name!

These first three commandments are similar in their intent. Amongst Semitic peoples a name, like an idol, could focus the power of a god and the person who knew a god's name could control that god's action. But Yahweh could not be used like that.

The fourth commandment required that one day in each week should be set apart by the Israelite community to remind them of their identity:

Remember to make the Sabbath Day holy!

27

Just as humans and objects could be removed from profane usage and rendered holy to Yahweh, so too a day could be removed from the profane usage of work and toil and rendered holy to Yahweh. The text continued:

> Six days you shall work and perform all your labour. The seventh day will be a Sabbath to Yahweh your God. Neither you nor your son nor your daughter, nor your male servant nor your female servant nor your cattle nor the stranger who is staying with you shall do any work.

In the Book of Deuteronomy the motivation for maintaining the Sabbath Day is humanitarian: the Israelites were once slaves and so they should grant their own servants a day of rest.

The Book of Exodus gives an alternative reason for this commandment:

> In six days Yahweh made the heavens and the earth, the sea and all that these contain, but he rested on the seventh day. Therefore Yahweh blessed the Sabbath Day and made it holy.

The other commandments referred to the life of the community rather than to Yahweh himself.

> Respect your father and your mother!

Israel's commandments were directed to adults and not children so this referred not to obedience of the young but to the obligation of adults to care for the helpless aged. All life within Israel was sacred. The motive for supporting aged parents was the fear that an abandoned and outraged parent might invoke Yahweh's curse on uncaring children instead of asking for his blessing and thus ensuring a long life for those children.

> In that way your days in the Land which Yahweh your God gives you will be long.

The community of Israel was dedicated to the principle of the sacredness of life.

> You shall not kill!

Murder for the Israelite was killing someone who was innocent in the eyes of the community. Killing in war or the execution of those under legitimate death sentence were not forbidden.

You shall not commit adultery!

Another short prohibition strengthened the marriage bond within the community. Israel did not require monogamy but by the Christian or Common Era it was the more regular practice. A marriage was arranged between the two families involved and from the time the arrangements were completed the betrothed couple were considered married according to the law of Israel. Divorce was allowed. Only an adulterous wife had to be divorced. Jewish scholars allowed divorce for various reasons but gradually detailed procedures were formulated in the hope that a long delay would bring about reconciliation. A wife could divorce a husband for reasons such as impotence or deliberately abandoning the home. The commandment protected the right of the husband to his marriage. No other Israelite should interfere with that right. In this way Israel ensured the stability of life within its community and the control of women and their reproductive powers. The commandment did not refer to sexual intercourse between unmarried people, nor to intercourse between a married man and an unmarried woman. It specifically forbade intercourse between a married woman and a man who was not her husband, whether he was married or unmarried.

While Israel did not condone any sexual activity outside of marriage this commandment sought to ensure that the family unit would be stable and that families would live peaceably with each other. It also sought to ensure that there would be no doubt over who was the father of a particular child.

You shall not steal!

Since a later commandment covered the ordinary instance of theft, there are those who consider that this commandment forbade kidnapping, the stealing of persons rather than things. Kidnapping in ancient societies provided a source of free workers. Israel maintained the rights of its members to personal freedom.

You shall not bear false witness against your neighbour!

This commandment did not generally exclude all untruth. It referred specifically to the question of legal justice. There was no police force in ancient Israel. Justice was rendered on the basis of one witness's evidence against a defendant, heard before the elders of the group. On the word of a neighbour an Israelite could be executed for a serious crime. If the community was to live as a covenant group then that legal basis had to be protected. Lying in a legal trial could not be tolerated.

You shall not covet the house of your neighbour . . .

Probably that was how the commandment originally stood. 'House' was a very broad term encompassing all of a neighbour's property. Later on, that property was enumerated more exactly:

You shall not covet your neighbour's wife, male servant or female servant, ox or ass, or any of the possessions owned by your neighbour.

'Covet' encompassed the whole range of meaning from planning to thieve to the actual accomplishment of the theft. The wife was included in the inventory as part of the husband's belongings.

The Ten Commandments, curiously enough, were not specifically mentioned by the early Christians. Jesus at times cited some of the ten but not in the above order, nor the ten of them in their entirety. Only at a later stage was the moral stance of Israel seen in the Ten Commandments. As they now stand in the biblical text they are an ethical basis for the way in which the Israelite should regulate life and behaviour towards Yahweh and towards the other members of the community. The Israelite community was one that accepted Yahweh as its only god, who respected his absolute freedom, not trying to manipulate or control him. Created by his free choice, this community responded by respecting the aged, life, the stabilising institution of marriage, personal freedom, justice and the property of others. These were the signs of a covenant community. They were signs that Israel was Yahweh's people.

A holy people

The morality of Israel was, therefore, a response to the action of Yahweh perceived in historical events. It did not develop from philosophical thought, but from life in action. As the Christian era approached, the Jews suffered many setbacks but could still find in the Torah a justification for their required response to Yahweh. Forced to mingle more and more with other peoples, they wished to manifest their election by Yahweh, the fact that they were a holy people. They saw their ethical system summed up in the book of Leviticus: 'You shall be holy, for I, Yahweh your God, am holy!'

Of all the nations of the world they were required to be the one special people of Yahweh. Other nations might be more politically powerful, more culturally advanced, but Israel was the Holy People of Yahweh. All their works and their style of life should reflect that holiness. From the time of the exile onwards, after the destruction of the city of Jerusalem by the Babylonians in 587 BCE, holiness became the dominant ethical interest. A new ethical programme laid down the prescriptions for a holy, moral life. Other nations must see holiness reflected in every action and word of Israel.

So the religious laws of Israel laid down directions for the external and physical expression of holiness. The body of the Jew was to appear as a perfect container. Any sexual emissions, even involuntary ones, as in the case of menstrual blood and semen, were considered violations of the laws of cleanness. People emitting them needed purification before they rejoined the community to worship Yahweh.

Every action should reflect the perfection of the holy Yahweh: the Jew was not to yoke different species of animals to the plough, nor to make cloth from two different kinds of thread. The Jewish diet was to consist of perfect food. Only animals that chewed their cud and were cloven-hoofed were regarded as being 'perfect'. Only sea creatures which had scales, fins and no legs were 'perfect' fish. Every meal, every enterprise of the Jew manifested the perfection and holiness of Yahweh.

The demands for holiness found in the book of Leviticus may now seem cold and unfeeling, but the Talmud, a collection of Jewish tradition composed in the fourth century CE, but drawing on much earlier tradition, shows how the life of holiness had warmth and caring:

> Rabbi Hama the son of Rabbi Hanina said: 'What does the verse mean which says "You shall walk after the Lord your God"? Is it possible for a person to follow after the *shekinah* [the divine presence] of which it is written "For the Lord your God is a consuming fire"? But the verse means that one should follow after the attributes of the Holy One, blessed be He: as He clothed the naked [i.e. Adam and Eve] . . . so you should clothe the naked; the Holy One, blessed be He, visited the sick [i.e. Abraham] . . . so you should visit the sick; the Holy One, blessed be He, comforted mourners [i.e. Isaac, who was mourning the death of Abraham] . . . so you should comfort mourners: the Holy One, blessed be He, buried the dead [i.e. Moses] . . . so you should bury the dead.'
>
> Talmud, Sotah 14a

The many codes of law within Israel—the Covenant Code, the Deuteronomic Code, the Ten Commandments, the Book of Leviticus—all showed ways in which the *'emunah* of Israel could be put into practice according to the different historical and cultural circumstances of Israel's life.

Jews have continued to deduce from the Torah with its various codes what is required of them in the practical day-to-day running of their lives. The rule of life is called the Halachah, but it is not contained in any one book. It is more like a collective wisdom that has grown over the ages and still continues to grow as new situations occur in Jewish experience. Experts in Halachah determine what is permitted and what is forbidden for Jews. Obviously there is not always unanimity even among the experts.

Relying on the Torah, the decisions of the Halachah experts, and everyday experience, Jews believe that God has given action-guiding commandments to Israel. These are called *mitzvot* (the singular is *mitzvah*). A *mitzvah* is a good deed commanded by God, who has indicated what activities are holy, just as he is the Holy One. Traditionally, Jews recognise 613 *mitzvot*. Sometimes these are listed under the headings of the Ten Commandments. Sometimes they are listed as prohibitions and positive requirements. Thus under the first commandment there would be the *mitzvah* to believe that God is one. A negative *mitzvah* would be the forbidding of pork as food; a positive *mitzvah* would be the requirement to recite the special Jewish morning prayer, called the *Shema*.

Pharisaic holiness

There was one group whose particular emphasis had a marked influence on Jewish ethics in the Common Era. These were the Pharisees, a group greatly misunderstood, particularly by Christians. Their origins were among devout students of the Law who perused the sacred traditions to make them intelligible to the common people.

When Jews revolted against persecution and repression by their Greek overlords in the second century BCE these scholars supported the revolution. The struggle against the Greeks, led by the Jewish family of Maccabees, was successful for a time but the Maccabees became too political, too involved in worldly aims for the pious scholars and they broke away.

From that breakaway group resulted the sect of Pharisees. Their name is something of a mystery; perhaps it means 'separated ones'. They advocated rigorous attention to the Torah, not only those laws and prescriptions that were written down but also those handed on by scholars from the time of the exile. This group of rules was known as the Oral Torah and was described as a 'fence built around the Torah'. Eventually Jews gathered all such rules, laws and ordinances into the Talmud.

Pharisees maintained that the true Jew was the one who knew and kept the 613 prescriptions and prohibitions of the law that were mentioned above. This observance made the Jew righteous before Yahweh. They established their own additional rules for the keeping of the Sabbath, the avoidance of unclean food and so on. And yet, despite such meticulous attention to detail, they were flexible. Relying on the Oral Torah, which could be adapted with time, they became the 'liberals' amongst the Jewish sects by the Christian or Common Era. They were open to new ideas and ready to reformulate old ones.

The Romans destroyed the city of Jerusalem completely in 70 CE and many Jews who survived the siege had to flee to other parts. Only the Pharisees survived as a vital Jewish force. By that stage a fierce enmity had developed between Jews and the newly formed Christian group. They engaged in debate and attacked each other bitterly. For the Christians, 'Pharisees' became synonymous with 'Jews' and when they wished to decry Judaism it was upon the Pharisees they poured scorn and ridicule. Even the Christian gospels contain traces of this attitude, and rejection of the Pharisees is even attributed to Jesus. The Pharisees' real contribution to the Jewish ethical system was clouded by this Christian view. Christians saw them as hypocrites who allowed the letter of the law to destroy its spirit. In reality, the Pharisees were not like that.

The law of Israel was not a backward ethical system. There was flexibility and warmth. In the first century CE Rabbi Akiba could write: 'And you shall love your neighbour as yourself—this is the main principle of the Torah.'

Jews lived amicably enough with non-Jews, stressing the need to avoid deceit in trading, respectful of the belongings of others, careful to preserve life and the reputation of others. In this way they continued to live out their response to Yahweh who had called them to be his people.

Medieval and modern Judaism

During the Middle Ages the Jews studied their ancient writings quite extensively. They showed great interest in the moral teachings of their ancestors and produced some fine treatises on the moral life. These writings had wide circulation and stressed the need for love and fellowship among all people, the need for purity in all human dealings, the need for honesty in all relationships. Gradually many saw in the ethical system of the Torah the basis for a way of life not only for Jews but for anyone who sought what was good.

What of Jews today? Those who adhere to the Jewish faith and base their life upon its demands still see their ethical system in the Torah. The Torah has come down to them both in its written and its oral form, with the accumulated wisdom of many centuries. Modern Jews recognise a long line of tradition from their ancient patriarchs through generations of pious scholars, wise people and Rabbis.

They are aware that no law can cover all situations; no moral code can foresee every contingency. So some general ethical principles are accepted, derived from the practice of the past. The first principle is that the need for justice is to be tempered by a merciful and forgiving attitude. On occasion, therefore, Jews may have to forgo what is rightfully theirs or extend themselves beyond the demands of duty. The second principle requires them to act with a piety that is beyond the minimum standard demanded of other people. They alone can judge this. The third principle is that Jews should act in such a way as to establish *shalom*, 'peace and well-being', among all people. Finally, all their actions must be pervaded with *rahmanut* or compassion, a merciful attitude that rules out cruelty.

The Jews of today still consider ritual requirements morally binding. These are part of their way of life. What they eat is a moral decision since food has been organised for them by God. Thus the Jew is still forbidden to eat unclean meat. Meat must be prepared under supervision to ensure that all blood has been removed because blood, being the source of life, is sacred to Yahweh. Three times in their ancient law codes the people of Israel were exhorted not to 'boil a kid in its mother's milk'. The original prescription probably forbade the use of a fertility rite practised by the Canaanites to ensure that the herd would reproduce. The prescription occurred three times because of the gathering together of various collections of laws. Jews of modern times have interpreted this prescription as demanding the complete separation of milk and meat dishes at table and in the kitchen. Tracing such practices can be interesting, but the important thing is that Jews, whether at table or about their daily work, are aware that they are to be holy, that they are to give evidence of that holiness, since their people have been chosen by Yahweh.

Modern Jews are particularly noted for their observance of the Sabbath. On the Sabbath they refrain from work and they rejoice. This joy reflects the Jew's certitude that the world is a good place; it is the creation of Yahweh. Jews continue to celebrate the great feasts of old. They celebrate Passover, recalling the Exodus from Egypt, together with the Feast of Weeks, reliving the experience of Sinai, and the Feast of Tents, which commemorates the great journey through the desert into the land. Some more modern feasts are the Jewish New Year, the day when all humans are called to account for the way they have lived and used their world, and the Day of Atonement, a day of contrition and repentance.

Modern Jewish morality is not confined to the purely personal. Jews see themselves responsible for the community in which they live. The needy and the poor must be cared for.

> All who occupy themselves with the affairs of the community should do so for the sake of heaven [i.e. Yahweh].
>
> Talmud, Avot 2

While such caring applies primarily to fellow Jews, it is extended to non-Jews who live with the community of Israel:

> Support the poor of the Gentile together with the poor of Israel, visit the sick of the Gentile together with the sick of Israel, and give honourable burial to the dead of the Gentile as to the dead of Israel, because of the ways of peace.
>
> Talmud, Gittin 61a

Orthodox and Reform

The modern era has seen Judaism divide into two principal groups: Orthodox and Reform or Liberal Jews. The background to Reform Judaism was the persecution of Jews in Europe when they suffered at the hands of Christians. After the Napoleonic wars, religious freedom and toleration spread and Jews at last received their full rights. They became more involved in civic life and a drastic change overtook them. Whereas they had found an identity in suffering common persecution, they now found it hard to remain united and true to their faith, when allowed their freedom. Many Jews abandoned the ways of their predecessors. Reform Judaism set out to adjust the practices of the ancient faith to the new situation, removing from Judaism anything that might stand as a barrier to social relations with the broader society. Dietary laws were not so exactly observed and the language of the people replaced Hebrew at worship.

While the basic ethical system remains the same the actual moral practice of Judaism differs in Orthodox and Reform synagogues. Orthodox Jews follow the laws and the practices that have come down from the past with a less questioning attitude than Reform Jews.

Jewish attitude to the environment

Jewish tradition has always seen the world as basically good. At the end of the creation story in Genesis 1 God surveyed his handiwork: 'God saw all he had made, and indeed it was all very good.' Jews have tended not to see anything inherently evil in the world. The world is there to be enjoyed in moderation. Jews have identified passages in the Torah which require people to take care of the earth itself. The law of the Sabbatical Year in the book of Exodus, for example, required that every seventh year the earth be allowed to lie fallow and rest. Just as humans rest on the Sabbath so the land must be given its rest. The Jubilee Law in Leviticus 25 demands that after every 49 years the land is to revert to its former owners. Yahweh's land was to be shared equally by all his people. If an Israelite was forced to part with land, it must eventually return to that person or to that person's family. No one could gain a monopoly on land ownership because Yahweh was the true owner of all land. Perhaps both laws were more ideals than realities but the idea underlying both is that the true owner of all land is Yahweh not humans. Israelites are simply tenants who manage the land for Yahweh.

However they have also recognised the fact that this good world has allowed evil to corrupt it. By the beginning of the Christian or Common Era Jews expressed their belief in the presence of evil by saying that evil demons inhabited the deserts and the seas. Evil demons could infect people too.

If the world is not, therefore, perfect then it can be improved. However improvement is not brought about only by physical means. The world is improved by the performance of good deeds. The performance of evil deeds aids and abets the powers of evil and makes the world a worse place in which to live.

One part of the world is particularly sacred to the Jew and that is the land of Israel. There is a *mitzvah* that requires all Jews to settle in Israel, although there are many obligations which would make such settlement impossible and those obligations excuse Jews from going to Israel. Still the religious ideal is to live in Israel. Many other *mitzvot* relate to life in the land of Israel which must be respected and made holy. Jews see a close connection between God, the Torah and the land of Israel.

We can deduce from this the modern Jew's attitude towards the environment. The world is a good place, created by God, but it can be improved. Humans have a right to interfere with it. At the same time the world must be respected. This is most true of the land of Israel and less true of the rest of the world.

Judaism and modern ethical issues

Some of the modern problems posed for Jewish morality have concerned medicine. One obvious case is abortion. The Torah does not specifically deal with the case of intentional abortion. Jewish scholars have, however, reflected on Exodus 21: 22:

> If men, in the course of a fight, injure a pregnant woman and she suffers a miscarriage although she does not die, then the responsible person must pay due compensation to the woman's husband.

From this verse Jewish scholars have concluded that the foetus is to be regarded as part of the mother's body, only becoming a separate person at birth (or even later according to certain Rabbis). Since it is part of the mother then it is the property of the husband and compensation must be paid to him. There can be no question of the murder of a foetus since the foetus is not a human person.

The fact that intentional abortion would not therefore be murder does not make 'abortion on demand' acceptable to all Jews. Orthodox Jews, in fact, invariably condemn abortion. They claim that the Jewish tradition has a deep respect for all life. While the foetus may only be a partial person it still has the potential to become a full human being one day.

The Liberal or Reform tradition tends to be more open and would allow abortion in those instances where the physical or mental health of the mother requires intervention. They would claim that the principle of respect for life allows some exceptions.

The general principle of deep respect for human life underlies other reasoning on medical ethics within Judaism. Medical experiments (for example on unborn foetuses) are allowed only where no injury is done and where life is likely to be enhanced. This principle is open to some interpretation. Jews believe that while there is a responsibility to preserve life it could happen, for example in war, that the whole community is threatened, and then the need for group protection may override the right of an individual to life. Sometimes Jews may kill. Likewise in other situations, the principle may give way to greater needs. It is in such cases that the Halachah is open to new developments and vital growth.

Jewish ethics and women

The covenant between God and Israel gave the Jewish people a special identity and a special purpose in history. There was a reason for Israel's survival and in order to ensure its survival a stable family life was required. The Torah presumes that male power is the means of family stability. A girl was seen as belonging to her father and he controlled her life. When she married she passed over to a husband's control and became his property. An Israelite woman served her husband, her people and her God by producing sons for the future of Israel. The sin of adultery was consequently understood as violating the property rights of a husband, if the woman was married, or the property rights of her father, if she was unmarried.

This subservience of the woman was written into their sacred text. The creation accounts in Genesis 1–2 reveal that men and women are complementary. In Genesis 1 God creates Adam as both a male and a female at the same time. In Genesis 2 God fashions Eve from the rib of Adam. Each fulfils the other; each has need of the other. But that is not how things are. The 'Fall' story of Adam and Eve in Genesis 3 shows that both male and female have missed the mark in life. Eve is intelligent and practical. She demands the fruit from the serpent because it is good to eat and the source of wisdom. Adam eats what his wife sets before him. Both contravene the command of God. The result is that the fulfilling, equal relationship of man and woman has been disrupted forever.

After the destruction of Jerusalem in 70 CE the Pharisees saw sexual sin as the principal way in which holiness would be sullied. It was said of women:

> Women are evil, my children. Since they have no power or control
> over men, they deceive by their physical appearance in order to
> attract men.
>
> Testament of Reuben 5: 1

The male was seen as the normal form of humanity, the
female was a deviation. She was only a peripheral Jew.
Women were therefore exempt from those *mitzvot* that
were tied to time since her time was to be given over to
husband, family and home. Hence she was not bound to
recite the morning prayer as was a man; she was not
bound to the Sabbath synagogue observance; but she was
bound by the negative *mitzvot*. She was not allowed to eat
unclean food; she was not allowed to tell lies or to steal.
The life of the woman was thus connected with the home.
She was obliged to provide for all her husband's physical
needs, and to enable him to study the Torah.

Feminist Jews have long protested against this. Their
voice has been stronger in Reform or Liberal Judaism than
in Orthodox Judaism. Reform Judaism has a stated commitment to women's religious equality. In fact since 1972
Reform Judaism has allowed women to be ordained as
Rabbis. There has been a call for the rewriting of the marriage ceremony so that the woman is not merely a silent
onlooker but a real participant in the ritual. Feminists have
asked that key moments in the woman's life be made
sacred by a ritual as happens in the life of a man. They
have also asked that women be bound by the same moral
demands as men.

Conclusion

For many people in the world today Judaism continues to
offer a fruitful way of life. By living out their response to
Yahweh they find that they can evaluate what is good,
what is right and what is wrong, what should be done and
what should not be done. Their ethical system however

cannot be dissociated from their experience and belief. It only has meaning when it is accompanied by the firm belief that the god Yahweh chose this people to be his, to be the light of the world, to be holy as he, Yahweh, is holy.

2
Christianity

The cross upon which Christ
died became the symbol of
Christianity because Christians
have seen in the seeming
defeat of his death the true
victory of humanity.

Main dates of Christianity

Birth of Jesus		CE
Death of Jesus		30
Letters of Paul	▼	50
Gospel of Mark		65
Gospels of Matthew and Luke		75
Gospel of John		100
Roman Empire incorporates the Christian Church		313
Rise of Papal influence	▼	600
Challenge from Islam		700
Eastern Orthodox and Roman Churches separate		1054
Christian Crusades against Islam		1100
Jan Hus, Czech reformer, executed		1415
Martin Luther rebels against Rome		1517
Emergence of various Protestant churches	▼	1600
Expansion of Christian missions	▼	1800
Formation of World Council of Churches		1948
Vatican II, Roman Catholic Ecumenical Council		1962

A new commandment I give you: Love one another.

Christianity

Neither Christianity itself nor the ethical system of Christianity can be understood in isolation from Judaism. In fact Christianity began as a sect of Judaism. The prophets of ancient Israel perceived the activity of Yahweh in the history of their people. They saw that Yahweh, the God of the Exodus, always acted according to the pattern of the Exodus. He always brought oppressed people, living in bondage, to freedom and new life. At any moment in Israel's history the people saw themselves as an oppressed people being led by a Moses along the Way. The Way, as outlined in the Torah, was the moral path of Israel. From about 1000 BCE, the Moses of the Exodus era was succeeded by the line of kings stemming from David. The prophets recognised the continuance of Yahweh's guidance and protection in each king as he assumed the throne. But not all the kings were faithful and the prophets looked more and more towards the future when they expected a king like David himself who would lead the people to a new freedom, throwing off the domination of foreign nations and restoring Israel to its former pre-eminence.

Jewish expectation

In 586 BCE the city of Jerusalem fell to the Babylonians and it soon became obvious that there would be no future kings from the house of David. Israel looked even more to the future, and the Jews felt sure that Yahweh would intervene. A *messiah* (*Christos* in Greek) would come, an

anointed one, who would rule as king. Jews often specu-
lated about the coming rule of Yahweh, which the Messiah
would inaugurate; a rule of righteousness, justice and eternal prosperity.

But conditions worsened. The Jews continued to be oppressed and even persecuted and they were persecuted
precisely because they would not deny Yahweh as their
god. This developed their religious beliefs. Earlier in their
history the Jews had believed that at death everyone went
down to Sheol, a shadowy cavern under the earth, where
they lived a life of drowsy awareness. It was not real living,
but it was not a place of pain. Those who followed the Way
of Israel had to receive their reward within the limits of
this life and the unfaithful could only be punished during
the reprobate's lifetime. Some Jews had certainly protested
that things did not work out in practice—that there were
faithful Israelites who suffered in this life and faithless
people who prospered. But their protests grew strident as
young Jews, who had never experienced the joy of living to
the full, who left behind no children to continue their name
and honour, died because they would not deny their al-
legiance to Yahweh. It did not make sense. From suffering
there was born a new way of thinking, and a new way of
writing that was called *apocalyptic*.

The two ages

This apocalyptic way of thinking made a distinction between *ha'olam hazzeh*, 'this age', and *ha'olam habbah*, 'the
age-to-come'. 'This age' was a period of lawlessness and
evil, over which the anti-Yahweh forces had control. But
there would come a time in the future when Yahweh
would usher in 'the age-to-come'. The concept was similar
to the earlier idea of the rule of God except that it stressed
the passing of this present age. It would be preceded by a
period of intense struggle, sometimes referred to as 'the
temptation'. Yahweh would send his Messiah to lead the

forces of good, the children of light, against the forces of evil, the children of darkness and, after a bitter conflict, the forces of good would triumph and the age-to-come would begin. But there was a problem: what of those who died in the final battle and what of the faithful who had died before the Messiah arrived? For the first time, in response to this problem, there was a breakthrough in Jewish thought on the future of humankind: the faithful would be resurrected. Yahweh would go down to Sheol and raise up the faithful. The victors in battle and the resurrected faithful would then share the rule of Yahweh, the everlasting age of peace. The wicked would languish in Sheol forever.

Spurred on by this apocalyptic mode of thought, the Essene sect of the Jews went to the arid fringes of the desert, around the Dead Sea, to an area known today as Qumran, in order to await the coming of the Messiah. They saw themselves as the nucleus of the children of light. They lived a devout communal life, and their ethical system was dominated by belief in the coming of the Messiah. In fact, they expected two Messiahs, a royal one and a priestly one. They consequently showed concern and offered companionship to their fellow monks and submitted to their Teacher who guided them while they waited for the Messiahs. But they had only hatred for the children of darkness with whom they would eventually do battle. The Essenes' monastery at Qumran was eventually destroyed by the Romans in 68 CE, around the same time as the city of Jerusalem was besieged.

Christians

There was another group whose origins were obscure but whose thinking parallelled that of the Essenes. In 35 CE or thereabouts they announced to their fellow Jews that the Messiah had actually come and, unexpectedly perhaps, he had been executed by crucifixion. He had been the first to be resurrected even while the final stages of the battle against the children of darkness were taking place. The age-to-come was about to dawn, they proclaimed. All who heard the message must join their group and be ready to greet the Messiah when he returned to gather together his faithful followers. These were the Christians, and their Messiah, or Christos, was Jesus.

Although the earliest Christians firmly expected that the age-to-come would dawn very soon, their expectations had to be modified as time passed and it became clearer that the end was not so imminent. The letters of Paul to various Christian communities give evidence of groups settling down, sometimes with reluctance, to a long wait. They were eventually to accept the inevitability of establishing structures of authority whereby stability could be ensured. Practices of worship developed into a distinctively Christian ritual and gradually creeds of belief, to which all Christians had to subscribe, circulated from one Christian community to another. The apocalyptic movement very quickly gave way to a stable society.

For the Christian group, the coming of Jesus changed the whole direction of Israel's history. They perceived, in their own time, a new Exodus, the passing from the oppression of this age to the newness of the age-to-come. Jesus was the new Moses who led his people in this Exodus which took the form of a battle with the forces of evil. He had died, but was the first to be resurrected and thus complete the journey. Others would follow. The Christians bestowed the new name of *Abba* or 'Father' on Yahweh who had wrought this wonder. Because Yahweh, or the Father, had acted in a new way, there was the possibility of a new response to that action and a new relationship. There was a demand for a new and higher righteousness. The Way of Israel, its moral path and its ethical justification, was to be replaced by a new path and a new justification. Thus we find in the earliest Christian writings talk of a *new* law, a *new* covenant, a *new* commandment, a *new* teaching. The

Way of Israel, the Torah, was said to have been reformed or replaced or fulfilled.

The early Christian ethical system

In the eyes of the Jews, the Torah had detailed the Way to Yahweh. Jesus replaced the Torah for Christians. Christian eye-witnesses recalled actions and sayings of Jesus which then became normative in the life of the group. Jesus' ministry of forgiveness, his healing, his bringing of light and peace to the needy, his unremitting judgement of evil and falsity became the exemplar for the lives of Christians. Jesus, throughout his life and in his death on the cross, had given himself totally in the battle of good against evil, in the Father's final endeavour to bring about the rule of peace and righteousness upon earth. Christians had to re-enact the self-giving of Jesus by their own love and forgiveness, patience, mercy, forbearance. Just as Israel saw its moral practice founded on a response to Yahweh's interventions in history, so the Christians saw their morality founded on the need to respond to the Father's action. The pattern of that response was laid down in the example of Jesus.

There was no place in the early Christian church for any systematic ethical theory. Christians simply lived what they considered to be the good life. At first, everyday life with its decisions over what was good and what evil, what was right and what wrong, was influenced by the belief that theirs was a time of crisis and that soon the age-to-come would be upon them. As the years passed and the End did not come, Christians began to consider particular moral problems and make explicit the ethical system of the community. The simple moral stance of the first Christians was expanded by codes of morality borrowed from society in general, detailing the domestic virtues that any close-knit society would require for survival.

Paul's ethical system

In order to review the moral character of the first Christian groups we must refer to the writings of the first community. The first writer we know of was Paul of Tarsus. He did not set out to write a treatise on Christian ethics, but he did attempt to regulate moral behaviour among the communities he directed. Paul believed that from the time of Jesus' coming, Yahweh had made a new relationship or covenant with humanity. The former covenant, as laid out in the Jewish Torah, could now be put aside. In fact, Paul maintained that if one looked back over Jewish history, it seemed that while Jews might have known what was good and right they were never able to do it. The Torah just did not give enough assistance to them. In fact, it made them appear guilty and rebellious. Naturally we must see what Paul said against the background of someone who was ungenerous to those Jews who did not convert to Christianity as he had done.

There was a new covenant with God. Christians who behaved like Jesus had more than an external law, like the Torah, to guide them. In some way Christians could be inwardly associated with Jesus, whose death would help them accept a Christian life of self-giving, symbolised by the Cross. The inward assistance of Jesus would destroy the very urge to sin. Jesus, working through the Spirit among Christians, would bring Christians, in an unforced way, to love others. Paul described such Christian love:

> Love is patient; it is kind. Love is not jealous; it does not put on airs. Love is not proud. Love is never unbecoming; it does not seek its own ends; it does not stir up anger; it does not seek revenge. It does not rejoice in what is not right, but rejoices in the truth. Love can put up with everything; it can trust to the end; it has infinite hope and it endures all things.

1 Corinthians 13: 4–7*

*All biblical quotations in this chapter have been translated from the Greek by the author.

Such love, patterned on the love of Jesus, was the ideal of the Christian. The Christian could perceive that the Father had acted in a new and definitive way in the life and death of Jesus. It was this perception, and the acceptance of what it entailed, that gave the Christian the power to share in the self-giving of Jesus. Faith, or believing in Jesus, had the very practical result of producing a special Christian love, an attitude of self-giving towards others. For Paul, it was this love that summed up all Christian morality. It was not so much that the Christian was commanded to do something new. The new element was the reason that justified such love—the self-giving of Jesus on the Cross. Jesus, who gave himself for others, lived on within Christians and caused them, quite spontaneously, to give themselves for others.

Paul insisted that the love of the Christian should be directed toward all humanity. It was not sufficient for it to be restricted to any one group. The rule of God was about to burst into the arena of world history. All humans were therefore neighbours to whom love must be shown by the Christians. In the new society there would be only one community. It would have no divisions and no barriers. The Christian Church, in Paul's vision, was already the nucleus of that new society and therefore there were demands made on Christians:

> Because of the favour extended to me, I say to each one of you not to esteem self above what is proper, but to esteem self with modesty in keeping with the measure of faith that God has apportioned to each one. Just as we have many members in the one body and all the members do not have the same function, so we are many but yet united bodily in Christ. As individuals we are members of one another. We have gifts according to the different favour bestowed on us. One might have the gift of prophecy within the limits of the faith. Another might have the gift of ministering and this should be used in self-giving. Another might have the gift of teaching and this should be used for teaching.
>
> Romans 12: 3–7

Paul's moral teaching was dominated by the continuing presence and action of Jesus amongst the Christians. Jesus had certainly died but he lived on, as it were, in the Spirit of God. It was this presence which made it possible for human actions and attitudes to be transformed. People could achieve what was good because of the inward power of Jesus that united them in the body-person of the Christian group. The loving community continued the self-giving of Jesus. Paul continually assured Christians that they lived 'in Christ'.

The essential ethical basis for Christian living is clear enough in Paul. When he descended to moral specifics he showed himself to have been a person of his own times. He accepted society, its institutions and outlook more or less as he found them. He tried to explain how a response to the Father, patterned on the living example of Jesus, could be lived out in the social circumstances in which his communities lived. Paul clearly rejected homosexuality yet he accepted slavery. He laid down guidelines illustrating how master and slave should express their Christian response, but he saw nothing unchristian in a master owning a slave.

> Slaves, obey your masters in all things. Do so not only when they are watching, just to gain their approval, but do it from a sincere heart, because of your reverence for the Lord.
>
> Colossians 3: 22

> Masters, be right and fair in the way you treat your slaves. Remember that you too have a Master in heaven.
>
> Colossians 4: 1

The difficulty inherent in transposing moral behaviours from Paul (or any New Testament writer) to modern life is clear. Society has changed and social attitudes have changed. Might a Christian response today call for different action from that practised by first century converts? Varying approaches are found among Christians in modern times. Some insist that the directives of the gospels and early Christian writings must be accepted at face value, quite literally. Others accept some moral directives literally and overlook others. Finally there are more liberal Christians who detach the underlying ethical reasonings of Paul, or other Christian writers, from the specifics and re-apply them to new situations in the world of today.

Mark's ethical system

We now turn to the gospels of the Christian church. The gospels were written at least thirty to forty years after the death of Jesus. They took on a written form only when it became clear that the end was not imminent and that there was danger of Christians straying from the truth. The gospel of Mark seems to be the earliest of the four gospels and it incorporates traditions about the sayings and actions of Jesus that had been circulating in the early church from the time of Jesus. Mark's gospel has little directly moral material. Its outlook is still coloured by the apocalyptic hope that the final consummation of all things will come soon. The principal duty of the Christian group was to implement the rule of God; day-to-day living was not considered in great depth.

An example of this outlook can be seen in the matter of divorce. In Mark the prohibition of divorce was absolute. It was intolerable in a community where the rule of God had been established and true peace reigned, that a man should divorce his wife.

> At the beginning of creation he made them male and female. Because of this a man will leave his father and mother and the two will become one person. They are no longer two but one. Therefore what God has joined let no one sever!
>
> Mark 10: 6–9

The language used was taken from the creation story in Genesis 2 depicting the ideal peace that humans could enjoy. But by the time of the gospels of Matthew and Luke, perhaps a decade later, there had been a change, as we will see below. Moral directives were not stated so generally or so absolutely. The Christian community was settling down to face a long period of waiting. Consequently there was the need for more specific rules of conduct, a clearer moral guide.

Matthew's ethical system

Matthew's gospel has such an ethical guide in the Sermon on the Mount. Sayings of Jesus that filtered down from earlier tradition were gathered together into a structured programme. The same sayings, in many instances, occur not only in Matthew but in Luke, although in scattered and different contexts. These sayings of Jesus and memories of his action were gathered by the early Christians due to various needs (such as instructing converts or combatting Jewish opponents in debate). How accurate the memories were we cannot, at this distance, be sure. The sayings ascribed to Jesus in Matthew are therefore more truly the moral statements of the first Christians.

In the Sermon on the Mount, Matthew produced an ethical justification for the early Christians, showing them how to act in a world that had been dramatically changed by the arrival of the rule of God. We will follow the Sermon section by section.

The Sermon on the Mount

The prologue to the Sermon consists of the Beatitudes. Various epithets have been taken from the sacred writings of Israel and applied to the Christian group in order to demonstrate the fact that they are the people who have entered the final rule of God. The Beatitudes stand as a proclamation that the way the Christian group live their lives is proof that the expectations of ancient Israel have been fulfilled in them.

Blessed are the poor in spirit because the rule of God belongs to
them;
Blessed are those who mourn, because they will be consoled;
Blessed are the lowly because they will inherit the land;
Blessed are those who hunger and thirst after righteousness, be-
cause they will have their fill;
Blessed are those who are merciful; for they will have mercy
shown to them;
Blessed are the sincere for they shall see God;
Blessed are the peacemakers, for they will be God's children.
Blessed are those who are persecuted for the sake of righteousness
for God's rule is theirs.

The Christian group are here described as the 'poor' of
Yahweh, those who have put their complete trust in him.
They are 'mourners' because they recognise the refusal of
the world to respond to the call of God. They 'hunger and
fast', in a ritual-prayer as it were, that righteousness might
be the common possession of all. They are the 'forgiven
ones', who subsequently extend that forgiveness to others.
They are 'sincere', one-minded, dedicated to the cause of
peace between humankind and God. Because of the stance
they have taken, however, they are also the 'persecuted'.
These Beatitudes announce that a new group has emerged,
the Christians, and they are practitioners of a new
righteousness.

The old and new

The first section of the Sermon then contrasts the old and
the new righteousness: the response of Israel to the initiative of Yahweh and the response of Christians to the initiative of the Father. A general statement assures the
Christian group that their righteousness fulfils the requirements of Judaism.

Do not think that I have come to do away with the law or the
prophets. I have not come to do away with them but to fulfil
them. For I say to you solemnly that until the universe passes
away, not one tiny letter nor one tiny stroke will disappear from

the Law until it is totally achieved . . . I tell you, however, that if your righteousness does not surpass that of the Scribes and Pharisees, you will not enter God's rule.

Matthew 5: 17–18, 20

Five concrete illustrations are then given showing how the new righteousness of the Christian group is superior to the righteousness of Israel. Each of the instances chosen stresses that the relationship between the individual and God has been deepened and internalised in Christianity. Thus, not only is murder forbidden in the Christian community, but any denial of family closeness, such as anger or disrespect.

You have heard that it was said to the past generation: 'Do not kill! Whoever kills will be answerable to the court.' I say to you that anyone who even becomes angry with his companion will answer to the court. Anyone who says to his companion: 'Fool' will go before the Sanhedrin and anyone who says 'Unfaithful Fool' will be liable to the fiery Gehenna.

Matthew 5: 21–2

Not only is adultery, which undermines the very stability of marriage, forbidden, but any lust which may detract from the intimacy of the marriage bond.

You have heard that it was said: 'Do not commit adultery!' But I say to you that anyone who even looks lustfully at a woman has already committed adultery with her in spirit.

Matthew 5:27–8

Not only is lying forbidden but even a lack of candour or honesty. Amongst Christians there should be, consequently, no need for oaths.

The law of retaliation, which moderated vengeance in earlier Israel, is replaced by a Christian demand for non-resistance to evil.

You have heard that it was said: 'Eye for eye and tooth for tooth.' But I say to you: Do not stand up against an evil person. If anyone strikes you on the right cheek, offer that person the other cheek as well. If someone takes you to court to sue you for your tunic, let such a one have your cloak as well. If anyone forces you to march one mile, go two.

Matthew 5: 38–41

Finally, the Christian group are given an ideal of universal love for all people, imitating the love of Jesus who gave himself for all.

You have heard that it was said: 'Love your neighbour and hate your enemy.' I say to you: Love your enemies and pray for your persecutors.

Matthew 5: 43–4

Christian ethical motivation

In a second section of the sermon, Matthew discusses the specifically Christian ethical motivation that should animate all moral practice. There is a stress on inward sincerity and inward involvement. Three examples are taken: almsgiving, prayer and fasting. Each follows the same format:

Take care not to perform your righteousness before others so as to attract attention. Should you do so, then you will not receive any reward from your Father in Heaven. So, when you give alms, do not blare it out on a trumpet as hypocrites do in their synagogues and on the streets, so that people will praise them. I say to you they already have their reward. When you give alms, do not let your left hand know what your right hand does, but let it be done in secret. Your Father, when he sees what has been done in secret, will reward you.

Matthew 6: 1–4

The sermon concludes with three admonitions addressed to the Christian group:

Do not judge!
The Christian who responds to the challenge does not sit in judgement on the response of another Christian.
Beware of false prophets!
The Christian must follow only one example, that of Jesus. False leaders will offer alternatives which must be rejected.

Be practical!
Once the Christian has seen the challenge of Jesus there should be no delay in responding. That is the only wise course of action.

The Sermon on the Mount offered the first Christians an outline of practical morality. It was not exhaustive but it did lay down a plan. Just as Israel had been called to respond to Yahweh and Israel's response was outlined in the Torah, so Jesus had been called to respond to the Father and his response was the new law. The new law did not abrogate the Torah of Israel; according to Christian belief it fulfilled it. Any Christian morality from that time onwards had to be based on the response of Jesus. The Sermon on the Mount gave ethical guidelines for imitating that response.

Luke's ethical system

Luke's gospel did not contain a separate section on moral behaviour. Although many of the sayings of Jesus found in the Sermon on the Mount are reproduced in Luke, they are scattered and in different contexts. Luke's gospel bases Christian morality on the example of Jesus who brought salvation and hope to humanity, who loved his neighbour, who lived his life and eventually died for the simple and the outcasts. Christians must live likewise. Luke stressed that the Christian's 'neighbour' is whoever stands in need. The story of the Good Samaritan made this point; it answered the perplexing moral question—who is the neighbour to whom the Christian must show self-denying love?

> A lawyer stood up and, trying to test Jesus, said: 'Teacher, what should I do to inherit the life of the age-to-come?' Jesus said to him: 'What is written in the Torah? How do you interpret it?' He answered and said: 'You shall love the Lord your God with all your heart and with all your spirit and with all your strength and with all your mind. You shall also love your neighbour as you

love yourself.' Jesus said: 'You have answered correctly. Act in this way and you will find real life.' But this person wished to justify his position and said to Jesus: 'But who is my neighbour?' Jesus gave him this answer: 'A certain person went down from Jerusalem to Jericho and was attacked by thieves. They stripped him, beat him up and went off leaving him close to death. It chanced that a priest was also travelling along that way and, when he saw him, he passed by on the other side. Likewise, a Levite also came to that spot, saw him and passed by on the other side. But a Samaritan, travelling the same route, came upon him and seeing his plight, was moved with compassion. He went to his aid and bound up his wounds, soothing them with oil and wine. He placed the man on his own mount and took him to an inn where he cared for him. The next day he produced two denarii and gave them to the innkeeper saying, "Take care of him and I will pay any expense incurred when I pass by this way again." Which of these three do you consider to have been a neighbour to the man attacked by the thieves?' The lawyer answered 'The one who took pity on him'. Jesus said to him: 'Go, and act in the same way'.

Luke 10: 25–37

Luke counselled Christians to act with generosity and he commended the practice of poverty. In an ideal depiction of the original Jerusalem community in the book of the Acts of the Apostles he presented an idyllic image of Christians who shared their worldly goods, shared their worship of the Father and gave common witness to the transformation that had taken place in their lives.

All those who had come to believe lived together and shared everything in common. They used to sell their property and goods and distribute the money so gained among themselves according to need. Daily they went together to the Temple. In their homes they celebrated the 'breaking of bread' [Eucharist], sharing their food in gladness and with simplicity.

Acts 2: 44–6

All those who had come to believe were united in heart and mind, and no one maintained that possessions were personal belongings. All was shared in common.

Acts 4: 32

John's ethical system

The gospel of John was the last of the gospels to be completed, possibly some decades later than the others. It shows significant differences compared to the other three. Most probably it was the gospel of a Christian community in Asia Minor, but behind the moral statements of John's gospel there stood a group who had come to terms with the apocalyptic delay. There are traces of the expectation that the end will eventually come. But there is evidence that the community believed the age-to-come was already being experienced, that the judgement, distinguishing the good from the wicked, was in the present. While other Christian groups saw the need for a missionary endeavour to announce the coming of the rule of God, the community of John considered that the division had already taken place. In their eyes, the Christian believer had no duty of love towards the 'world' outside. The 'world' had had its chance but had rejected the opportunity. All ethical duty related to the restricted group of the saved. Thus, in John the terminology of 'love' took on a new connotation:

> Little children, I am with you only for a little while . . . I give you a new commandment—that you love one another. Just as I have loved you, so you must love one another. Everyone will perceive that you are my disciples by this—that you have this love for one another.
>
> John 13: 34

> Do not love the world nor anything in the world. If anyone loves the world, the love of the Father is not in that person.
>
> 1 John 2: 15

The inward turning morality of John's gospel and his letters is accompanied by a stress on the role of the Holy Spirit who is given the name of Paraclete, which means something like 'Comforter'. 'The Holy Spirit' referred to the dynamic aspect of Yahweh. In the period prior to the Christian era some of the Jews had awaited a forceful manifestation of the power of Yahweh, which they called the Holy Spirit, without intending to indicate any being other than Yahweh himself. The Holy Spirit would renew the vitality of God's people and would destroy their enemies.

John's gospel announced that after the death of Jesus there had been the manifestation of the Holy Spirit. Jesus had instructed his disciples; the Spirit would instruct all the Christian group. Jesus had comforted and protected his disciples; the Spirit would comfort and protect all Christians. All this was summed up in the epithet applied to him—the Spirit of Truth. 'Truth' was a technical Jewish term describing the final unveiling of the work of God to humanity. When people saw Truth they would see all that could be known of Yahweh and what he could accomplish amongst them. They would know the fullness of response that he was demanding. Jesus, in John's gospel, had identified himself with this Truth. He was the Truth of Yahweh, the Father. But the opportunity would be given to everyone to perceive the Truth in the activity of the Holy Spirit:

> I have many more things yet to say to you but you are not able to cope with them. But when the Spirit of Truth comes, he will guide you to all Truth. He will not speak on his own account, but he will speak of what he hears and will announce what lies in the future.
>
> John 16: 12–13

The Holy Spirit was the tangible and active presence of the Father in John's community. John's Christians claimed to be aware of this presence and their morality was built on their response to it.

Modifying ideals

Having surveyed the earliest Christian writings we can conclude that there was basic agreement that the moral life of Christianity called for a response to the Father who had challenged humanity in the life and death of Jesus. But there were also considerable differences amongst the various communities as to the way this response was to be lived out. It is important to see how the earliest communities moved from the ideal to the practical. Perhaps the clearest example of this is the problem of divorce. We have already seen that Mark's gospel stated the ideal of a Christian group which awaited the end. Divorce had no place amongst Christians who lived in the final peace of the rule of God. But as time went on the communities had to cope with the realities of marriage breakdown. Matthew's gospel virtually quotes that of Mark but allows a loophole:

> It was said 'Whoever would divorce his wife, let him give her a bill of dismissal'. But I say to you that anyone who divorces his wife (except in the case of *porneia*) makes her an adulteress and whoever marries a woman who has been set free in that way commits adultery.
>
> Matthew 5: 31–2

Unfortunately we do not know today what *porneia* meant. Certainly it had a sexual connotation, perhaps adultery, perhaps a forbidden degree of kinship. The important point is that, in the community of Matthew, the original moral directive had been modified due to practical necessity.

Paul compared the marriage bond to the relationship between Jesus and the Church. Yet Paul also included in his correspondence an escape clause. In his first letter to the Corinthians he wrote of the case of a Christian, newly converted, who was married to a non-Christian. If after conversion, the Christian could not find peace because of difficulties caused by the non-Christian partner, then the Christian could divorce the partner.

The issue of divorce shows how the early Christian church developed its moral teaching. It began, in the context of apocalyptic thinking, with a statement of ideals for those who awaited the final manifestation of the rule of

God. The ideals were adapted from the Torah of Israel and the practice of Jewish life. Jesus' own teaching must have given the lead. The moral teaching was modified and amended as problem cases were proposed in various Christian communities. The ethical system could be adapted.

Christian divisions

Christianity did not remain unified. The most noticeable division was between the East and the West—the Greek Orthodox Church formally split from the Western Catholic Church in 1054. However, a rift had developed long before then. Each of the two churches had gone its own way. The Greek Church had used Greek as its sacred language in ritual; the Western Church used Latin, the language of the Western Roman Empire. The Greek Church looked to the Patriarch of Constantinople for leadership; the Western Church insisted that the Bishop of Rome, the Pope, was spiritual leader of all Christians. Different practices and customs, different ways of expressing Christian teaching led to an estrangement.

The influence of the Greek Orthodox Church had spread far. Missionaries had been sent to the Slavonic people such as the Serbs, the Bulgarians and the Russians. They became Christian in the Greek tradition. Russia is an interesting case. Prince Vladimir of Kiev (980–1015) is said to have dispatched messengers to observe Jews, Western Christians, Eastern Christians and Muslims at their worship. In the great Orthodox cathedral in Constantinople the messengers thought they were in paradise as they saw and heard the beautiful liturgy of the Greek Church. They related their experience to Vladimir and he determined that his people would become Greek Orthodox Christians. This was the beginning of the Russian Orthodox Church.

There were to be further divisions. In the West a major

split took place in the sixteenth century. Over a long period there had been considerable unrest, and many in the Western Church felt that the teachings of the Church needed to be reformulated. They believed that the ritual had become too formal and too removed from the needs of the people, and that authority had been usurped by the Pope and those who surrounded him. Reformers like the Englishman John Wyclif (1329–84) called for a return to the simple teachings of the Bible. He influenced a Czech priest, Jan Hus (1374–1415), who also stressed that the teachings of the Bible were the supreme authority in the Church. Hus was burned at the stake when he tried to explain his views at a Church Council. Then in 1517 Martin Luther, a monk and priest, challenged the authority of the Pope. Luther was excommunicated and he, with a large following in Europe, established what they saw as a reformed church. This was the beginning of the Reformation and of that form of Christianity known as Protestantism.

Other reformers now asserted themselves. John Calvin in Geneva and Ulrich Zwingli in Zurich were important names. In England, Henry VIII, having been denied a divorce by the Pope in order to marry Anne Boleyn, removed the Catholic Church in England from the control of the Pope. Over several decades this was to lead to the establishment of the Anglican Church.

Meanwhile the Roman Church itself underwent an internal reformation. A Council met at Trent and between 1545 and 1563, in three sessions, it eradicated many of the abuses decried by the Protestant Reformers. This renewed church was the Roman Catholic Church.

The following chart gives some idea of the divisions down to our own day.

Divisions of Church to our day

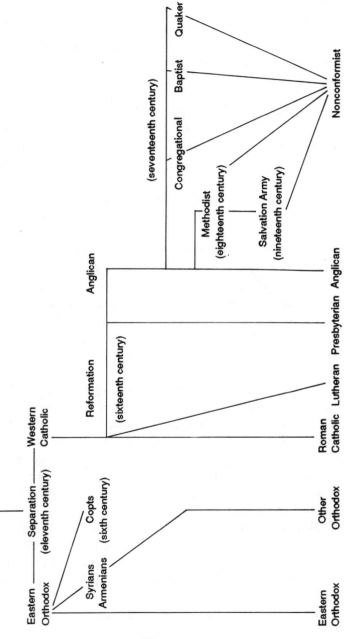

Christian ethics and the many Christian churches

How have these changes in the organisation of the Christian churches affected Christian ethics? We have seen that there has been, in the course of history, a splintering of the Christian Church. Each resulting group has tended to go its own way. In time, these groups have produced various Christian teachings. They have also produced various ethical systems. We can identify three main factors which have influenced ethical reasoning in the many Christian Churches.

In the first place the attitude of Christians to the rule of God has differed. The coming of the end has retreated more and more into the background of Christian thought. It is sometimes reinterpreted as the ongoing activity of the Father who continues to challenge humanity. Because of this, it is said, the Christian cannot know, in advance, what a Christian response to a particular life-situation should be. Only when the Christian is actually in the situation, faced with the action of the Father in life, can a Christian response be made which is authentically a manifestation of love.

Christians also vary in their understanding of human nature. For some Christians the human person is unchangeable, unvarying. For others the human person cannot be regarded as substantial and predictable and therefore Christian morality cannot be unchanging. The latter group see the ethical system of the New Testament as indicating only a general direction; its specific moral directives are not normative.

Thirdly, Christian groups look to one or other authority for their ethical reasoning. For some it is the Bible alone. For others it is the tradition handed down from the past and, perhaps, explained by a leader such as the Bishop of Rome.

Thus, we can try to summarise the ethical system of the

Orthodox Christian Churches. While we recognise that there are differences among various Orthodox churches we find that, in general, they stress their reliance on biblical authority. They are proud of the fact that their behaviour is principally regulated by the Ten Commandments and the Sermon on the Mount. They tend to disapprove of trying to split hairs and using human reason in justifying their behaviour. The biblical text should be sufficient. Certain characteristics of their moral behaviour have been described by their scholars. Their lives, it is said, should be noted for *agape*, a love that mirrors the love of God for all others, for its *creative suffering*, sharing the struggles of others, not separating themselves from anyone, and for its *kenosis*, patterned on Jesus who, as Paul said, 'emptied himself and took on the role of a slave' (Philippians 2: 7).

We will now look, in particular, at the development of the ethical system in the Roman Catholic Church, and in passing at the Protestant Churches that make up the balance of the Western Christian tradition.

Roman Catholic ethics

The Catholic ethical system owes its origins to the Middle Ages. At that time the writings of Greek philosophers, including the ethical writings of Aristotle, were studied by Christian scholars. Thomas Aquinas made use of Aristotle's ethics to re-express the Christian ethic of the Western Church. Aristotle had based morality upon the rational person's search to attain the supreme good. When rational people consciously sought the means to attain that supreme good, they did good things. Otherwise they did evil. Aquinas simply substituted Christian terms for those of Aristotle. He spoke of people seeking to attain the vision of God or salvation, and claimed that the means of arriving at this supreme good were moral works.

According to the medieval theory, these moral works

were governed from both within the human person and from outside the human person. Within were ingrained habits, called virtues, such as prudence and justice and charity. The human being was assisted in acting morally by these habits. However other habits could lead the person away from a right path. These were called vices. From the outside, the individual was directed along the path to the supreme good by the law of God which was accompanied by God's directing assistance. This law was known as the eternal law directing all creatures, and indeed all creation, towards their proper end. Non-rational creatures follow the law blindly. Only rational creatures can resist it, to their own detriment.

From the seventeenth century the Roman Catholic Church's ethical reasoning took a new turn. More stress was by then placed on the practical training of its clergy. They were required to make practical decisions for their people as to which actions were allowed and which forbidden. The textbooks used in educating the priests of the Catholic Church concentrated on an image of the human person that was regular and unchanging. It was claimed that absolute norms of behaviour could be formulated, based on the eternal law and on the teachings of the Bible. These norms presupposed that there was a constant and harmonious moral law that could be known. Because of this moral law what was right and what was wrong could be objectively determined in every instance. If a clash did seem to be present it was simply due to human ignorance. This moral law was applied to particular cases by conscience.

By this time the morality of the Catholic Church was being derived from a variety of ethical sources: the Bible, Councils of the Church, decrees of Popes, Code of Canon Law, works of the Fathers of the Church, works of moral theologians, use and practice of the Church. As with all religious traditions, Catholicism found moral dilemmas and seeming moral impasses. Could a pregnant Catholic woman have a cancerous womb removed if it would mean aborting the foetus at the same time? If a Catholic persuades a friend not to steal $100 from X but to steal instead $20 from Y, has that person done a good thing or has that person wronged Y? All dilemmas, it was said, could be solved by certain principles. First, if a Catholic had doubts as to what was demanded by a moral law, that Catholic could follow a 'probable opinion', a liberal view based on good argument and scholarship. If the difficulty concerned evil consequences that followed an activity that was good then the 'principle of the two-fold effect' allowed the performance of an action from which followed immediately two effects, one good and one evil. The evil effect was tolerated only.

Always the Catholic could be quite certain about what was to be done. Never could a Catholic be objectively faced with a situation in which all options were evil. If, in fact, this seemed to be the case then the Catholic was obviously in error and could choose what seemed to be the least evil alternative according to the principle of 'invincible ignorance'.

These three stratagems ensured that the moral system was clear-cut and absolute. There were no exceptions. The Catholic culture was constructed on a Greek concept of the natural law. It was believed that there is an order of things which defines human beings as humans; the natural law is outside of humans and must be followed. In addition, because humans have been raised to a supernatural calling, there is a divine law they must discover and follow. Because Jesus established a Church and gave it authority, the Church established ecclesiastical law. Such absolute laws gave certainty.

Then, a revitalising movement aroused Catholicism. In 1962 Pope John XXIII announced that he was convening a new Council, to be called Vatican Council II. All Catholic bishops, together with non-Catholic observers, were to attend. Its purpose was to renew the Catholic Church, re-express its teaching and re-consider its ethical stance. Vatican II brought about wide-ranging reforms and changed the face of the Catholic Church. Not all Catholics approved of its changes and not all Catholics have followed the new ethical directions since that time.

Some more liberal Catholics have rethought the natural law concept; they see it as being not outside human beings but within them. Human beings define themselves, and personal responsibility is emphasised. While values (such as the dignity of human life) may be absolute, the norms used to achieve them (such as the prohibition of killing) were relative to the particular historical situation.

This fundamental change of perspective caused some Catholics to question ethical sources of behaviour. For example, even if the text of the Bible condemned homosexuality, some said, it also condoned slavery. Some Catholics said Popes had expressed the limited vision of their time. In other words, all sources would be relative to a particular time and context. It has been claimed by some Catholics that only the individual Christian participating in a concrete, historical situation could make an absolute ethical judgement regarding behaviour. Not all Catholics came to such a conclusion and there are liberal-minded Catholics who find themselves at odds, over ethical theory, with the official Church.

Protestant ethics

The Protestant Churches had a variety of ethical systems. Amongst them there has always been a great reliance upon the teaching of the Bible on moral behaviour. However this biblical approach also allows considerable variation, depending upon the extent to which that teaching is taken literally. In recent times the Catholic Church has also turned more to the Bible and the two major Christian traditions in the West have consequently come closer in their ethical teaching.

Both the Catholic and the Protestant Churches have stressed the biblical concept of 'love' as the ethical foundation for morality. Increasingly it has been said that Christian love, with all its dimensions of caring, compassion and self-giving, cannot be made into a fixed law. Since it is directed towards a neighbour, it will vary infinitely even as the notion of neighbour varies infinitely.

In modern times the Protestant Churches have put more and more stress on social justice in the world. They claim that the Christian ethical system can bring about a harmonious balance within society today. This trend is also more and more apparent in the Catholic Church. Accepting the fact that different Christian Churches have different approaches to moral problems, we will isolate three areas that are of common concern to the Churches today.

Christian attitudes to the environment

How does the environment fare within Christian ethics? Traditionally, Christianity has based its attitude towards the environment on Genesis 1: 26–8:

> God said: 'Let us make Humanity according to our own image, to our own likeness. Let them be in control of the fish of the sea, the birds of heaven, the cattle, all the wild beasts and all the reptiles that crawl over the earth.' So God created Humanity in his own image; in the divine image he created it; he created them as a male and a female.

> God blessed them and said to them: 'Be fruitful, multiply, fill the earth and take control of it. You are the rulers of the fish of the seas, the birds of the skies and all living animals on the earth.'

This text was accepted by the early Christians as proof that nature was not only a resource to be utilised to the best advantage, but something that needed to be subdued.

Human ingenuity could devise any technology for that purpose.

Christians have had to radically change their thinking in recent times because of problems such as pollution, soil degradation and the so-called 'green-house effect'. They have gone back to the biblical sources and found texts that extol the beauty of all creation, teachings that call for the protection of the environment. It is a commonplace for Genesis 1: 27–8 to be counterbalanced by Genesis 2: 15: 'Yahweh God took Adam and settled him in the garden of Eden to cultivate it and to take care of it.'

Humans are no longer proprietors and dominators. They are now said to be stewards or caretakers. A new ethical reasoning demands accountability of Christians as good stewards. A good steward will not accept the build-up of toxic waste or pollution by fossil fuels. That is not a responsible way of taking care of the garden.

There are some Christians, however, who do not think that even the 'steward' image adequately covers the tenor of the biblical writings. The biblical message of Genesis is reinterpreted so that the whole section of Genesis 1–2 is seen to insist upon the innate goodness of the world. Such goodness is independent of and prior to the existence of human beings; creation exists to glorify God and not to serve the human race. Psalms which call on the earth to praise God would seem to support this viewpoint.

Creation, these Christians would say, is valuable not because human beings need it; it has value because of its relationship to God. This forms the basis for a new environmental ethic. Since creation manifests the very presence of God it is to be trusted and its internal order respected. Human beings must learn to interrelate with the environment and so discover the wisdom and harmony given it by God. Human beings must then pattern their lives on what they find.

This is a drastic change in thinking. The new environmental ethic (also called a 'land-ethic') requires Christians to cease thinking in terms of land-use. The earth does not belong to them; they belong to the earth. Instead of being rulers of the earth, using it for their benefit, they are exhorted to see themselves as lovers and co-creators of the world.

Recently, the General Secretary of the World Council of Churches encouraged Christians

> to call on the whole human family to strive for the preservation and restoration of the natural environment—especially the world's animals and plants—interrelated with each other and with us...This can only be done by awakening countries and nations to seek justice and peace for all. They must also adopt policies and life-styles which model our responsibilities under God towards our human neighbour, all our fellow creatures and the whole of creation.
>
> Emilio Castro, World Environment Day Message, 1988

Women and Christianity

Within Christianity there have been two conflicting views on the status of men and women. One view sees men and women as equivalent human persons; the other defines women as subordinate to men, each having distinctive (and sometimes complementary) roles. This second view is based on the idea that God established a patriarchal social order. Patriarchy means that males are superior and must be respected for that superiority. Male headship, therefore, was seen as part of the order of things. Any attempt to upset this order (by giving women equal rights) would be a rebellion against God and would inevitably bring about chaos in society. A Christian ethic based upon this viewpoint requires women to be subject to their fathers and husbands. They must accept male rule even though that rule is usually softened by kindliness and love. The reason for the subordination and the consequent inferiority of women is the fact that woman was the originator of sin in the world.

The first viewpoint, where males and females are equivalent, is based on texts like Genesis 1: 27 where both male and female are created in God's image and form one person. That ideal image is said to have been restored by Jesus' coming amongst humanity.

> There are no longer any distinctions between the Jew and the non-Jew, the slave and the free person, the male and the female. All of you are united in Jesus Messiah.
>
> Galatians 3: 18

Whereas there were Rabbinic texts that thanked God that the person praying was male and Jewish, those Christians who hold to the equivalent viewpoint maintain that in Christianity all has been changed. In Acts 2: 17 the spirit of prophecy was given to both the female servants and the male servants. There is no longer any discrepancy.

But what of the undoubted moral statements in the New Testament that call for a wife's subordination? These are dismissed as the old patriarchal religion rearing its head.

Those who believe that men and women are equivalent claim that early Christianity addressed itself to the 'poor'. The 'poor' included not only those living in poverty, but also the ritually unclean and the non-Jews. It also included, they claim, women. Early Christians, they contend, would have welcomed women as the equal of men just as they welcomed the other outcasts as the equal of the socially respectable. Thus the Martha and Mary story in Luke 10: 38–42 is said to assert the woman's right to study the new Torah of Jesus. This is contrary to the traditional role of women in Judaism where they were supposed to cook and serve and so release males to study the Torah at leisure. The equivalent view would maintain that, some time later, the early Church accepted the patriarchal position. Any attempt to reassert the proper place of women in the Christian Church was resisted. In the Western Church the Protestant Reformers adopted the patriarchal tradition and enjoined silence and submission on women. Martin Luther asserted that even though males and females had been equal in paradise, woman was made subordinate as a result of her leading role in sinning.

> The wife should stay at home and look after the affairs of the household as one who has been deprived of the ability of administering those affairs which are outside and concern the state...In this way Eve is punished.
>
> J. Pelikan (ed.), *Luther's Works*, vol. 1 (Concordia Publishing House, St Louis, 1958), pp. 202–3

In short, the question arises—should patriarchy influence ethical reasoning?

In modern Western Christianity conflict has once more broken out. Some Christians maintain that subordination is the true and original Christian stance. They revive the argument that since Jesus was male and chose male disciples all priests and ministers should be men. Men have a place of privilege and superiority in the Christian Church. Women have, accordingly, a moral obligation to accept their subordination, to obey husband, father and male superiors. But there is increasing pressure by feminists to gain full equality within the Church and remove any moral obligations which are based on gender. Feminists claim that there are biblical arguments in favour of women's equality and that reason itself demonstrates that gender differences are culturally determined. While there are obvious sexual differences between men and women, gender is determined by culture and can change. Equality and non-equality of men and women are cultural perceptions. The various denominations of Christianity have reacted in different ways to the conflict, some accepting women into the priesthood and some continuing to follow the traditions and conventions of the past.

Christianity and modern ethical issues

One area in which the Christian ethical position is prominent concerns human sexuality and reproduction. Christians have usually regarded sexuality as a gift of God to be cherished and enjoyed. We have seen that the Genesis text instructed humanity to be fruitful and multiply. However the Bible did not give a detailed treatise on sexual ethics and did not foresee some of the more modern developments that affect reproduction. Christian ethical justification has relied heavily on the Natural Law theory. As we have already noted, the Natural Law is that rule which, it is said, all human beings are bound to follow. Moral behaviour, required by this Natural Law, is said to be justified by human reason reflecting on human nature, on what it means to be a human being, and which then determines appropriate human behaviour. The Natural Law presumes that human nature has certain goals and purposes towards which humans are naturally oriented and towards which human actions should be directed. The goals are good; actions directed towards those goals are good; any interference in the process is morally wrong and reprehensible.

One such goal is human reproduction. Sexual activity in line with procreation is good. Because the sexual organs are for procreation, the theory maintains, God and nature designed procreation as the end result of their use. Sexual activity directed towards procreation, carried out within the stabilising confines of marriage (necessary for the upkeep of subsequent children and the satisfaction of the two partners) is good. If procreation is impossible in a certain instance (when one partner, for example, is infertile) then sexual activity can still be good if it is directed towards the secondary purpose, the fostering of mutual and exclusive love between husband and wife. More recent writings would prefer not to use 'primary' and 'secondary' purposes but see the two forming a unity. Any interference with this linking of sexual activity to procreation is regarded as wrong.

Premarital sex is therefore wrong because it is not carried out in the necessary environment, the loving and stable family unit. Contraception and masturbation are wrong because they frustrate the purpose of the sexual activity. Homosexuality is rejected for the same reason. In this case Paul's First Letter to Timothy 1: 10 gives added weight when it condemns 'sodomites' along with a list of others who are regarded as evil-doers. Romans 1: 27 is also cited.

Not all Christians accept this ethical reasoning. In particular there are some who debate the reality of the Natural Law. They would say that there is no such thing as a 'human nature' that is static and unchangeable. Therefore, they would say the homosexual cannot be classified as 'unnatural': homosexuality and heterosexuality are two forms of human behaviour. Individual Christians must always grapple with the problems of individual life, so it would be impossible to predict what ethical choice should be made, in a particular and individual case, as to the rightness or wrongness of homosexuality.

Similar discussion surrounds the ethical goal of preserving of human life. It clearly excludes the intentional and wanton killing of people. But there are exceptions to a general rule. Many Christians justify killing others in a just war or in the execution of criminals for certain despicable crimes. But what of abortion, the intentional termination of a pregnancy involving the death of the foetus? Some more liberal Christians would say that the issue is complex. A woman who is pregnant has other duties to consider—to herself, her partner, her family, society and the world. A choice for abortion would be the last choice, the choice to be avoided if at all possible. But there may be compelling ethical reasons (for example, other children may suffer irreparably if she gave birth to a defective child) why that choice for abortion should be made.

Euthanasia poses a similar moral dilemma: whether the killing of those who are incurably ill or experiencing unbearable pain and wish to die is right or wrong. Conservative Christians would denounce any form of euthanasia as contrary to the goal of preservation of human life. Other Christians make distinctions. Some would say that if death is near and certain, if extraordinary measures are needed to preserve life and permission has been given by the patient or the patient's relatives, then it is acceptable. This is passive euthanasia, refraining from doing anything which would keep the patient alive. Other Christians again say that it is not simply the preservation of life that is the goal, it is the preservation of an acceptable quality of life. Where life is not worth living they would even allow, with adequate safeguards, active euthanasia, taking positive action designed to kill the patient. Obviously this would be in an extreme case.

New medical technology has opened up new challenges. *In vitro* fertilisation has offered hope to the childless. Conception can take place outside the womb and the human embryo can be implanted in the future mother's womb. Sperm may or may not belong to the male partner; the ovum may or may not belong to the female partner. Christians are perplexed. There are many issues which make the ethical debate complex: the question of ownership of embryos; the high cost of medical procedures which lessen the possibility of research in other areas; the high failure rate including the death of embryos; experimentation on embryos not required for implantation. Christian statements on the new technology range from outright condemnation to a limited acceptance.

Conclusion

There has been, and still remains, great variety in the theory and practice of Christian ethics. All Christians would agree that a Christian ethic must be patterned on the response of Jesus to his Father. That response is seen to reach a high-point in his self-giving on the cross. But from that point the traditions divide. Some rely on the authority of the Bible alone, as individuals interpret it. Others rely on the authority of a church community. Others look to other sources. There is no one Christian ethical system.

3
Islam

The crescent is a common
religious symbol earlier
associated with moon-worship.
It was taken over by Muslims
after they had conquered
Byzantium in 1453 CE. Since
then it has been accepted as a
symbol of Islam, especially in
Arab countries.

Main dates of Islam

		CE
Muhammad's birth		570
Muhammad's call		610
The Hijra		622
Fall of Mecca		630
Muhammad's death		632
Conquest of Syria by Islam		642
Ali as caliph		656
Shiah sect founded	▼	660
Conquest of North Africa		670
Conquest of Spain		713
Sufi movement	▼	800
Al-Ghazali, Muslim philosopher, reconciles Sufis and Orthodox		1000
Christian crusades against Muslim Turks	▼	1100
Turks capture Constantinople		1453
Turks take Syria, Egypt, most of Arabia		1517
Majority of Muslims under Western rule		1850
Rise of modernist and reformist movements in Islam		1900
Break-up of Turkish empire		1919
Abolition of caliphate		1924
Muslim states founded	▼	1950

Serve no other gods besides Allah.

Islam

The religion of Islam began during the seventh century CE in the western section of what is today Saudi Arabia. The word *islam*, 'submission', describes the basic attitude of the religion. Its founder, Muhammad, did not consider himself to be establishing a new religion but to be restoring and completing a very ancient one. He maintained that the true and only God, Allah, had revealed himself in ancient times to Abraham, the patriarch of Judaism, and then to the other prophets of Israel, including Jesus, the greatest of all the prophets prior to Muhammad himself. However, it was Muhammad's contention that both Judaism and Christianity had strayed far from the law of God, first revealed through Abraham. The prophets and Jesus had been sent by Allah to restore the original faith, but they were unsuccessful. Finally, the greatest and last of the prophets was Muhammad. Islam therefore saw itself as the fulfilment which both Jew and Christian, the People of the Book as Muslims called them, had awaited.

> People of the Book, why do you argue about Abraham when both the Torah [of Judaism] and the Gospel [of Christianity] were not revealed until after his time? ...Abraham was neither a Jew nor a Christian. He was an upright person, one who had surrendered himself to Allah. He was not an idolator. Those who are nearest to Abraham are those who follow him, the Prophet [i.e. Muhammad] and the believers [Muslims].
>
> Sura 3

Jews, Christians and Muhammad

Muhammad would have had only indirect contact with the sacred writings of Judaism and Christianity. Any knowledge he possessed of the two religions seems to have derived from stories that circulated by word of mouth in his society. To compare narratives that occur in the sacred book of Islam with those in the Jewish and Christian sacred books shows notable discrepancies. The omissions are also of importance. If Muhammad had access to the writing of the prophet Amos or to the Sermon on the Mount in Matthew's gospel he would surely have used them. It seems reasonable to suppose that Muhammad heard stories and knew of traditions relating Jewish and Christian teaching but did not have the actual writings before him.

Like the earlier religions Islam maintained that God, Allah, is creator and lord, that he has revealed a law, that he has sent prophets to speak to humankind, that he will be its judge, that he will reward the righteous in Paradise and punish the wicked in Hell.

Beginnings of Islam

In order to review the ethical system of Islam it is necessary to study the history of its beginnings. A religion does not start in a vacuum; it begins in a particular political, social and religious setting and this influences its development.

Islam came to birth in the vast expanses of the Arabian peninsula. The people had attained a high degree of culture in the southern region, particularly in agriculture and trade. A series of states had been established and they were ruled by priest-kings, political leaders who were also religious leaders. By the seventh century there were many fine temples, luxurious castles and an intricate system of dams to provide water for irrigation. The religion of these southerners included many gods but there were three in particular—a moon god, a sun goddess and another god who was probably the star Venus. Sacrifices were offered to these gods at due times and pilgrimages made to their temples.

In the northern section of the peninsula, however, a more ancient way of life had been preserved, although by the seventh century it was on the point of disintegrating. The ancient form of society was based on the tribe rather than on a political state. Stability was maintained by tribal solidarity, members of a tribe knowing that they could rely upon others within that tribe. This loyalty to one another was the essential quality of tribal life and it was known as *muruwwa*. The idea can be described as 'bravery, patience, protection of the weak'. The Arabs associated with it another term, *hamasa*, 'fortitude'. Tribal life was arduous and demanding. Fortitude was necessary for all people in the tribe to play their part to the full. If it came to pass that the rights of anyone were trampled upon, then the tribe took vengeance into its own hands. *Muruwwa* demanded that.

Tribal honour was the supreme ethical motive for doing good and avoiding evil. It determined the distinction between right and wrong. Tribal poets sang of the mighty deeds of the past and those deeds became examples for subsequent generations. The poets also sang of the evil deeds performed by other tribes. Listening to these songs from childhood the Arab learned to discern the good and the right thing to do.

This northern section also had many gods, but by the seventh century there were some religious preachers who proclaimed that the most important god was *al 'ilah*, 'The God', whose name was shortened to Allah. Allah lived in the sky and he provided rain and fertility for those on earth. A tree or a rock, surrounded by a sacred enclosure, marked a place of worship. Arabs who wished to worship and respect a particular god met at this place to eat a sacrificial meal. Pilgrimages were made to the sacred places at specified times of the year. The northern tribes, unlike the more sophisticated peoples in the south, had no organised priesthood. They did have sacred persons, however, who were known as *kahins* or 'prophets'. These people were able to see and hear things that others could not. Under the inspiration of a god they chanted in rhyme and sang to others of what they had perceived. Tribespeople listened to these prophets with awe and reverence.

At the end of the fifth century CE the area around Mecca had been seized by a tribe called the Quraysh. They made Mecca their religious centre and they honoured a shrine in the city called the *Ka'aba* or 'cube', built around a large black stone. The shrine housed several images of their gods.

By the seventh century CE this form of tribal life in the north was breaking up. Trade from the south was channelled through Mecca, the birthplace of Muhammad, and Mecca was enjoying a new prosperity as a result of this commerce. The merchants of Mecca, who came from a tribal background, forgot their tribal ties and ideals. People felt they must look after themselves and the greatest value was no longer the *muruwwa* of the tribe, but increased wealth.

Mecca was still governed in name by the tribal leaders but there was a growing tension between the wealthy traders and the smaller traders and workers. New wealth had brought an entirely new social system and the old ways of the tribe were not able to cope with it.

Muhammad

Somewhere around 570CE a child was born into the Quraysh tribe. This was Muhammad. Born in Mecca, he was orphaned early in life and then brought up by his grandfather and an uncle. Little is known of his childhood, most of the accounts being legendary. He entered the service of a widow named Khadija whom he eventually married and with her had a family.

Around the age of forty the life of Muhammad was dramatically changed. Tradition tells that he went to a cave on a hillside and there spent long hours in meditation. During one religious experience Muhammad was confronted by the god, Allah. Sometimes the confrontation is spoken of as a direct one, at other times Muhammad is said to have spoken to Allah by means of the angel Gabriel. Whatever did happen the experience transformed his life. Later, he was to describe the words he heard:

> Recite in the name of your Lord who is creator.
> He created humanity from a blood-clot.
> Recite! Your Lord is the Most Generous One,
> Who has taught humanity by the pen what it did not know.
>
> Sura 96: 1

After this call by Allah, Muhammad became a preacher. He was certain that he proclaimed not his own ideas but the message of Allah. The divine call impelled Muhammad to speak out and he became a *rasul*, an apostle to all mankind.

The call of Allah directed Muhammad towards a new way of life with new ideals, but he did not completely reject what had previously been acceptable in the life of the tribes. At first Muhammad attracted only close friends. His new way of life was generally despised and ridiculed by the Meccans. Even his own clan, within the tribe of the Quraysh, was unsympathetic. After all, he criticised the gods of Mecca and thus attacked what people valued most dearly. He preached the oneness of Allah and the need for social justice and threatened dire punishment for those who refused to hear. Muhammad appeared as a direct threat to the traders who had vested interests in the commerce of Mecca. Facing constant rebuff, he almost succumbed when his wife, Khadija, died. She had been a support to him amidst all his setbacks.

The Hijra

In 622 a group came to Mecca from a town to the north called Yathrib. They heard Muhammad preach his message and they were impressed by his inspired words. They returned to Yathrib and told their fellow citizens what they had heard. Muhammad was invited to come to Yathrib and become its religious and political leader. Controlling Yathrib was no easy task: the three thousand inhabitants were divided into two hostile Arab tribes and there were also Jews, who lived on the fringes of society. No central authority was able to unite the groups and order was only maintained by the fear of violence and bloodshed. Muhammad was asked to heal the wounds of long enmity and to form a community.

His journey from Mecca to Yathrib has been known to the Muslims ever since as the *Hijra* or emigration. It marked the beginning of Islam as a popular religion. By leaving Mecca Muhammad broke with the old tribal organisation and established his religion with its own institutions. This new organisation was the *umma* or 'community' of Islam. From this moment the inspired sayings of Muhammad changed in character. They became more concerned with the running of a society with its own internal problems and adjustments, with adapting that society to a new ideal. From this time onwards Yathrib became known as *medinat annabi*, the city of the Prophet, or just Medina.

The community which made up Islam was divided into several categories. There were the Companions, the privileged earliest associates of Muhammad who had followed him from the time of his call. There were the Exiles who had shared the emigration to Medina. Finally there were the Helpers, the people of Medina and those who had joined him after the emigration.

Growth of Islam

Life in Medina had its difficulties. There were economic problems and threats from the people of Mecca. In 624 Muhammad led a raid on a Meccan caravan at a place called Badr. The rage of the Meccans and the Quraysh exploded when the small group of Muslims were victorious. Subsequently, more followers flocked to Muhammad, but in the following year he was defeated at Uhud, not far from Medina. This caused a problem for the Muslims. If Badr had been a sign of Allah's protection how could the defeat at Uhud be interpreted? The answer stressed the principal element of all Islamic religion—submission.

> If you have suffered defeat, so too did the enemy. We change the fortunes of all humankind so that Allah can discern the true believers and choose martyrs from you...
>
> No one dies unless by permission of Allah. Every life's term is fixed. Whoever wants a reward in this life can have it, but whoever wants a reward in the life to come can have that, too. We will certainly reward the faithful.
>
> Many great armies have fought side by side with their Prophet. They were not daunted by what happened to them or the path of Allah. They did not weaken or fall back. Allah loves those who are determined. Their only cry was: 'Lord, forgive us our sins and our wasted efforts! Make us steady on our feet and give us victory over unbelievers.'
>
> As a consequence Allah gave them a reward in this world and a reward in the life to come. Allah loves those who do good.
>
> Sura 3: 140–8

Already the outline of the Islamic religion was taking shape. There was an order of things fixed by Allah to which Muslims must submit themselves. They did this by following the path of Allah. The struggle between Medina and Mecca soon came to a head when the Quraysh and their supporters attacked Medina. A tradition relates that there were 10 000 soldiers, Meccans and disenchanted Jews massed against the Prophet. Muhammad made use of trenches to disable the cavalry of the Meccans and the battle, won by Muhammad, became known as the 'Battle of the Ditch'. Mecca and Medina then made a truce for ten years.

During these years of uneasy peace, more of Muhammad's time was taken up with the problems of everyday life. Moral directives for living were devised to enable the people of Medina to live out their submission and surrender to Allah. Then, in 630, the period of peace ended when the Meccans attacked a Muslim tribe, thereby breaking the truce. Muhammad gathered his forces and marched on Mecca. The Meccans, seeing that they were surrounded, surrendered and Mecca fell into the hands of Muhammad. At once he enforced the observance of Islam. He destroyed the images within the Ka'aba but retained the structure as the centre of his own religion. The community of Islam, which had taken root at Medina, now included Mecca. Muhammad returned to Medina where he died in 632. By that time Islam was a religion on the march, incorporating the remaining tribes of the Arabian peninsula and moving towards the borders of the Byzantine Empire.

To the people of his time Muhammad offered a religion of obedience and submission to Allah. The moral practices upheld in the tribes of the Arabian peninsula were contained now within a framework of Islamic rituals and social behaviours. This is what Islam calls 'what is right'. In Arabic 'what is right' is the same as 'what is known'. What is known is right; what is unknown is wrong. The true path is that which has come from the past. So it is written:

You are indeed the best community that has ever been produced among humanity. You demand that what is right (or known) be done; you forbid what is wrong (or unknown) to be done.

Sura 3

The Pathway to Allah

Islam attracted peoples and communities. It called them to submit themselves to Allah. The whole way of life of these communities, their moral behaviour, was intended to put that submission into practice. The Muslim needs to know what must be done in order to live a life absolutely surrendered to Allah. So the law of Islam is called the *shariah* or 'pathway'. This Pathway regulates the Muslim's whole life, not only in matters of public order but also private morality, etiquette, personal hygiene and religious ritual. The Pathway is the means by which the guidance of Allah is made as explicit and detailed as possible. By following that Pathway exactly the Muslim becomes pleasing to Allah. What justifies the Pathway? Muslims name four ethical sources to which they turn in order to justify their human behaviour. The first and most important is the *Qur'an*, 'reading' or 'recitation'.The others are the *Sunnah* or 'custom' of Muhammad, the consensus, and analogy.

Qur'an

The Qur'an is the written record of the revelation of Allah to Muhammad during his lifetime, from his first call to be an apostle until his death. Muslims revere the Qur'an as the book of Allah himself. They consider that the book is without error; it cannot be questioned. The arrangement of material in the Qur'an does not follow any particular order. The longer suras or 'chapters' have been placed towards the beginning although they seem to have derived from the later period of Muhammad's life.

Muslims explain that the Qur'an was transcribed from tablets in heaven. The written contents of those heavenly tablets were recited to Muhammad by the angel Gabriel while the prophet was in ecstasy. Muhammad himself was passive, adding nothing and subtracting nothing. The place of the Qur'an in Islamic society differs from the place of the Torah or Bible in a Jewish or Christian community, which usually attributes certain ideas, or at least the expression of the ideas, to the human author. In Christianity it is said that 'the Word became Flesh'; in Islam 'the Word became Book'.

The principal affirmation of the Qur'an, which underlies all of the suras, is that Allah is one, and only he is to be worshipped. The worst sin that a person can commit is *shirk*, giving Allah a partner. In order to avoid any semblance of idol worship Muslims forbid the use of statues, images and pictures. Their mosques are notable for their artistic austerity with geometric designs or flower symbols as the only decoration. Allah is the God of judgement, dispensing rewards and punishment on the Last Day of which Muhammad gave warning. At the same time he is trustworthy and forgiving. Every sura of the Qur'an except one bears the title: 'In the Name of Allah, the Compassionate, the Merciful'. The attitude of Islam towards Allah provides an ethical foundation for Islamic moral practice.

The Qur'an continues to uphold the tribal *muruwwa*. Muslims must see themselves not just as members of a limited tribe but as part of a vast Muslim world. Muhammad took over the tribal ethical system which demanded equity, hospitality and just dealing and applied it, on a broader scale, to the whole of Islam. But he also made further moral demands on the Muslim.

Among the tribes, responsibility for exacting vengeance belonged to the kinship-group of the victim while responsibility for the crime fell on the whole of the culprit's kinship-group. Sometimes tribal law had allowed a substitution; for example, a hundred camels might be exchanged for the life of one guilty person. But many of the tribes frowned upon such innovations, particularly if the slaying was deliberate. The Qur'an encouraged Muslims to accept substitution in all cases.

> Believers, you may take retaliation for death: a free male for a free male, a slave for a slave, a female for a female. If a person is pardoned by the aggrieved party then that person should be prosecuted in the usual way and heavily fined. The Lord in his mercy has decreed so. Whoever offends again, however, should be punished severely.

When someone is clearly killed by accident, substitution was, in Islamic law, obligatory.

> It is against the law for a believer to kill another, except in the case of an accident. Whoever accidentally kills a believer must free one Muslim slave and then pay a fine to the victim's family, unless they choose to give it away as alms. If the victim is a Muslim from a hostile tribe, the penalty is the freeing of a Muslim slave. If the victim is a member of an allied tribe both a fine must be paid and a Muslim slave set free. If the offender cannot afford to do this, then that person should fast for two consecutive months. This is Allah's penance and he is wise and knows all things.
>
> Sura 4

The Qur'an stands somewhere between the ways of tribal society and the new individualism of Mecca's commercial society. While the law of retaliation still stood, there was a new stress on individual responsibility. Eventually, everyone would have to answer personally on the Day of Judgement and the tribe would not be able to cover over an individual's guilt.

The Qur'an also introduced the need for forgiveness, an ethical concept that the harsh laws of the tribes did not encourage.

> Obey Allah and the Apostle so that you will be granted mercy. Compete, one against another, to earn your Lord's forgiveness and a Paradise that is as vast as the heaven and earth. It has been prepared for the righteous: those who give alms in good times and bad, those who curb their anger and forgive their neighbour. Allah loves the charitable.
>
> Sura 3

95

The morality of the Qur'an reveals Muhammad's attempt to put submission to Allah into practice and to establish the Muslim society as a practical reality. Within the Qur'an no detailed code of morality stands isolated as do the Ten Commandments or the Sermon on the Mount. However, some sections of the Qur'an do give specific ethical guidelines.

> Serve no gods except Allah. Otherwise you will be disgraced and ruined.

> Your Lord requires you to worship only himself. Show kindness to your parents. If either or both of them grow old in your house, do not be impatient with them, do not rebuke them. Speak only with kindness to them. Treat them with humility and tenderness. Say: 'Lord, be merciful to them. They nursed me when I was still an infant.' Your Lord knows quite well what is in your hearts. He knows if you are good and he forgives those who turn to him.

> Give your dependents what they require and give to the poor and the traveller. Do not waste your money, for the wasteful are on Satan's side and Satan never recognises the Lord. However if you do not have the means to assist others, since you are still waiting for the Lord to enrich you, then at least speak kindly to them.

> Don't be either a miser or a spendthrift. The former would bring you a reproach and the latter would bring you to poverty.

> Your Lord gives abundantly to those he selects and sparingly to others. He knows and watches over his followers.

> You shall not kill your children for fear of poverty. We will provide both for them and you. To kill is a terrible sin.

> You shall not commit adultery. That is reprehensible and disgusting.

> You shall not kill any person whom Allah has forbidden you to kill, unless there is a just cause. If a person is unjustly killed, that person's heir is entitled to some return. The heir should not revenge the death since that victim will then, in turn, be avenged.

> Do not interfere with the property of orphans until they reach maturity, unless it is in their best interests. Keep your promises. You must give an account of all that you promise.

Give full measure when you measure out and use just scales. That is fair and will work out better in the end.

Do not follow what is unknown. A person's eyes, ears, heart, all the senses will be questioned.

Do not walk proudly on earth. You cannot open up the earth nor can you rival the height of the mountains.

All this is evil and hateful in your Lord's sight.

These commandments are only a part of the wisdom which your Lord has given you.

Serve no other god besides Allah. Otherwise you will be cast into Hell and left despised and helpless.

Sura 17

The Sunnah

While the Qur'an is the principal source of Muslim ethics, it does not cover all circumstances of life. After the death of Muhammad a new source was required to give direction on various moral questions that had no answer in the Qur'an. This was the *Sunnah* or 'custom' of Muhammad. The Sunnah itself was composed of *hadiths*, 'traditions', relating actions of Muhammad. One tradition told of Muhammad's reaction when a baby wet him, while another promoted the cleaning of teeth after a meal in the name of the Prophet. These traditions had been handed on by word of mouth and they consisted of two parts—a *matn*, 'text' and an *isnad* 'foundation'. The tradition gained its authority from a chain of 'transmitters': A told me that B said that C had informed him that D related that he heard E say that he heard F ask the Apostle of Allah about...

During the two centuries after the death of Muhammad there was both dissemination and fabrication of such traditions. Muslims with a cause invented a tradition to support it. Islam was faced with the need to distinguish between true and false traditions. The foundation for each tradition was carefully examined by Islamic scholars and each one was declared to be sound, good or weak. From this scrutiny there emerged six collections of traditions known as the Six Sound Books. They contained a few thousand of the hundreds of thousands of traditions that had been in circulation.

The consensus

But Islam discovered that even after examining the first two ethical sources, the Qur'an and the Sunnah, or collections of traditions, there was still doubt sometimes as to the proper way of proceeding in life. In such a case the Muslim would have to consult the *ijma* or 'consensus' of past generations of Muslims. If public opinion of the Muslim community, as expressed by Islamic jurists, agreed upon the rightness or wrongness of a practice then that opinion was upheld, provided it did not conflict with either the Qur'an or the Sunnah.

Analogy

Only when all three of these sources failed to provide an answer to a moral problem could the Muslim turn to the final ethical source in Islam—*qiyas*, 'measurements or analogies'.

Qiyas established a parallel between a moral teaching in the Qur'an or in the Sunnah and a new set of circumstances. It moved from the known to the unknown. Thus, for example, the Qur'an prohibited the drinking of wine because of its intoxicating effects. Therefore *qiyas* forbids the use of other modern drugs and intoxicants. Naturally it could happen that, after some time, a decision based on *qiyas* would be generally accepted by Muslims and taught by their jurists. In that case it would have the force of *ijma*.

The four ethical sources of Islamic moral teaching establish for the Muslim the shariah, the Pathway to Allah. The shariah is the way decreed by Allah. Muslims by their own reasoning cannot determine what is right and what is wrong; Allah decrees what is right and what is good. This divine authority is the first characteristic of the Pathway.

The five pillars of Islam

Another characteristic of Islam is the inclusiveness of the Pathway; there is no aspect of life that is left untouched. Even if, in some particular instance, there should be doubt about what Allah demands, there can be no question that one particular action is right and all others are wrong. The Pathway lays down two main spheres of duty. The first contains the duties towards Allah himself, called by Muslims the Five Pillars of Islam, five basic activities by which the Muslim shows surrender to God.

The first pillar is the profession of faith. This is the proclamation that Allah is God above all and that Muhammad is his prophet. The proclamation is the rallying cry of Islam, the announcement to the world made several times a day in Muslim countries from each mosque.

Prayer is the second pillar. A very physical type of prayer is required, a physical act of worship. Five times in the day the Muslim is expected to face towards Mecca and, either alone or in a congregation, to go through a ritual of prayer which expresses in both word and action the surrender of Islam towards Allah.

The same submissiveness is expressed in a third pillar, almsgiving. A definite proportion of each Muslim's income should be given to support the Islamic community. As Muslims go about their business they also distribute money to beggars.

A fourth pillar is fasting during the holy month of Ramadan. From dawn to sunset the Muslim should refrain from eating, drinking, and sexual intercourse.

> Believers, you are bound to fast just as those who came before you were bound. Fasting will guard you against evil. Fast for a certain number of days. If someone is ill or making a strenuous journey then that person can fast for a similar period later on. For those who can afford it there is an alternative—feeding a poor person. Whoever spontaneously does a good action will receive a fitting reward. Yet, if you only knew it, fasting is better.
>
> In the month of Ramadan, the Qur'an was revealed. It is a book that gives guidance and demonstrates what is right and what is wrong. Hence, all should fast during that month. Those who are ill or on a journey should fast for a month at a later date.
>
> Sura 2

The final act of submission is the pilgrimage to Mecca. At least once in a lifetime Muslims are expected to make the journey during the twelfth month. There they perform a ritual recalling the beginnings of the Islamic religion.

Duties towards others

Besides these duties towards Allah the Pathway also lays down duties towards others. Individual, social and political moral behaviours are subsumed under this heading. The Qur'an and the Sunnah outline the individual and social morality required for the right maintenance of Islamic society. Justice tempered by forgiveness, truthfulness, sexual integrity and compassion are enjoined. The Pathway is believed to cover all human activity and so all human actions are divided by Muslim jurists into five categories. An action may be obligatory, such as confessing the unity of Allah or performing the Five Pillars, or recommended, or permitted, or disapproved but not forbidden or, finally, absolutely forbidden.

The Shia

When Muhammad died he left no obvious successor. The Muslim group was therefore led by Muhammad's father-in-law, Abu Bakr, who took the title of caliph or deputy.

Under his leadership Islam continued to spread—into Syria, Palestine, Iraq, Persia and Egypt by means of the *jihad*, 'striving', or holy war against unbelievers. According to Muslim belief Allah ensured victory in the holy war and the whole enterprise was regarded as a sacred ritual. The fourth caliph was Ali, a cousin of Muhammad who was forced into a struggle for power with the governor of Syria, Mu'awiya, of the Umayyad tribe. In a battle on the Euphrates in 657 an indecisive Ali submitted to arbitration. Some of his adherents considered this a betrayal of Islam and seceded. One of these *Kharijites* or 'Seceders' assassinated Ali, and Mu'awiya became caliph after Ali's son abdicated. From this point the Umayyad tribe ruled Islam from Damascus for some considerable time.

At the same time a split developed amongst Muslim adherents. There were those who accepted the Umayyad rulers and others who thought that the caliph should be a direct descendant of Muhammad. At Mu'awiya's death one of Ali's sons, al-Husain, sought to regain the caliphate but was murdered. Ali's party then broke away and it became known as the Shia or 'Following'. What had begun as a political and social division took on a religious character.

In this way two major religious groups have emerged in Islam. The majority follow the Sunnah or tradition handed down from the past, principally in the Qur'an. They are called the 'people of the Sunnah' or Sunni Islam. The minority group is called Shia Islam or the Shi'ites.

The Shia began to elaborate their own teaching and their own ethical system. Sunni Islam, or traditional Islam, maintained that all knowledge from Allah and all direction about moral practice ceased with the death of the prophet and the writing of the Qur'an, but the Shia held that divine guidance was still available through descendants of Muhammad known as imams or leaders. These could reveal, without possibility of error, the inner meaning of the Qur'an and could add to the revelation from Allah.

Most Shia followers belong to a group known as the Twelvers. They recognise twelve such imams from Ali to Imam Zamam, 'the Imam of All Time', a young lad who disappeared in Iraq in 878. The Twelvers believe that he will reappear one day as the Mahdi, the Guided One. This is the state religion of Iran today. Other Shia groups acknowledge seven imams or four imams and there are innumerable sub-groups within the major divisions.

The principal difference in moral practice is that sayings and directives of the imam have ethical authority for the Shia. The effect of this differs from community to community, but to outsiders the life of the Shia appears very similar, in its moral demands, to that of Sunni Islam.

The Sufis

A more distinct ethical variation is found in the Muslim groups that tend towards mysticism. The term mysticism describes an ecstatic encounter, when the divinity seizes the religious person directly. It might seem that Islam would be exempt from such familiarity and intimacy with the divinity since it stressed humankind's distance from Allah, and the need for very concrete prescribed acts of piety in submission to him. But in the period after the Umayyads assumed the caliphate, many Muslims became more and more disenchanted with the worldliness and luxury of the court of the caliphs and they reacted against the many political and religious dissensions which were rending the Arab world. They were not satisfied with the arid piety then being practised. Accordingly, from about the first century after the establishment of Islam, certain Muslims sought within their religion a more personal and spiritual way of life.

An ascetic movement, which renounced the worldly values of the Umayyads, began in Iraq. Its members were known as *sufis* because they originally wore a coarse *suf* or woollen garment. They showed a contempt for the world and its pleasures and spent their time repeating litanies of phrases such as 'Allah' or 'There is no God but Allah' over and over again. This repetitious prayer was known as a *dhikr*, a 'remembering', and the Sufis felt that in this way they were able to keep the presence of Allah directly before them. A new religious spirit developed. A Sufi poet could write of her relationship with Allah:

> I love thee with two loves, love of my happiness
> And perfect love, to love thee as is thy due.
> My selfish love is that I do naught
> But think on thee, excluding all beside;
> But that purest love, which is thy due,
> Is that the veils which hide thee fall, and I gaze on thee.
>
> Rabbia Adnawiyya

The ascetic piety of the Sufis gave birth to a more ardent love of Allah who had seemed so far distant. Sufis desired above all to be at one with Allah, to know him personally, and they sought, by means of various *dhikrs*, to develop techniques that might accomplish this union. The ethical system of the Sufis differed somewhat from that of other Muslims. Whereas Muslims in general aimed at absolute submission within the community of Islam, the Sufis aimed at personal union with Allah. The Sufis were more demanding in the renunciation of the pleasures of the world.

From the twelfth century outstanding Sufi mystics surrounded themselves with disciples, and communities of mystics arose. The members of these communities were known as *dervishes* or 'beggars' and, since a teacher designated a successor within a particular group, a line of continuity was established. Just as the Shia looked to the imam, so the Sufis looked to their leader who became the director of their moral lives. The leader, *shaykh* or sheik, became the model of how life was to be led, since divine light shone through the sheik. The sheik required surrender, love, and trust. Often fasting, silence, or solitary meditation were enjoined on the followers. In this way the lower human instincts were curbed and the human person filled with Allah-like qualities.

The Sufis emphasised the spirit of the law, the feeling beneath the practice. They added to the moral practice of Islam a sensitivity that was being lost. An uneasy alliance was forged between the Sufis and the majority of Sunni Islam.

Islam's attitude to the environment

Islam has never taken an individual stand on ecology. It inherited the common teaching on creation from Judaism and Christianity. In this, humans were the rulers of the world. Added to this was a lack of interest in the world as such. For Islam the world is a passing phenomenon. Allah was depicted, from the first experiences of Muhammad, as the Judge. He would come on a Day of Judgement and divide all humanity into righteous and wicked. The wicked would be consigned to the Fire or *Jahannam*. The righteous would enjoy a physical Paradise, outside of this worldly sphere. At death the body, which was designed for earthly pursuits, decomposes but the soul develops the faculties appropriate to life in the world to come. Its birth into this new life is what is meant by resurrection. Awaiting the Day of Judgement and the subsequent resurrection the soul is like an embryo in a womb.

While the joys of Paradise will be intensified, Hell will not be permanent. Muhammad spoke of a time when Hell would be emptied, when torment would have achieved its purpose in curing the evil tendencies of the sinners. A blessed humanity will then reflect the qualities of Allah.

The focus on the hereafter has meant that Islam has lacked interest in the human body as such. It is the vehicle for life in this world, discarded at death. Likewise this world is the context for Allah's subjects to live out their submission. It too will be discarded. Such an attitude is unlikely to generate ethical sensitivity to ecological issues.

Women in Islam

The place occupied by Islamic women in their religion is always a matter of some debate. There are those who point to the fact that Islam raised the status of women considerably above what it had been in the pre-Islamic period. They recall that Islam banned female infanticide, gave women the right to inherit property and at least curbed the practice of polygamy by limiting a man's possible number of wives to four. Others see the present state of women in Islam as deplorable and calling for immediate protest.

The ethical sources controlling the moral behaviour of women are the same as those for Islamic religion generally. Naturally, the principal source is the Qur'an. Certainly, at first sight, the Qur'an seems to propose that males are superior to females. It states:

Men have a status above that of women. Allah is mighty and wise.

Sura 2

Men have authority over women because Allah has made the one superior to the other. Besides, men spend their wealth to maintain women. Good women are obedient. They keep their unseen parts safe because Allah keeps them safe. If you fear that a woman will be disobedient, then admonish her and send her to her room alone and then beat her.

Sura 4

As explicit as the texts seem, Muslims explain that men have been given the responsibility of taking care of women. Hence they have gained a certain authority over them.

It is possible to isolate four areas where Islamic moral practice impinges on women. The first is marriage. While a Muslim man is permitted to marry up to four wives provided that he treats them all equally, a woman can have only one husband. That husband must be a Muslim, while the wives could be Muslim, Jewish, Christian or even slaves. Within marriage abortion has traditionally been forbidden; it is seen as murder. Likewise birth control has been forbidden on the rather obscure basis of sayings in the Qur'an such as 'Marry and reproduce so that I can be proud of you before Allah' (Sura 2). However some modern Muslim jurists have allowed birth control on the basis that the situation of Islam has changed. In its earliest days it was necessary for Islam to spread and therefore children had to be produced in large numbers. Birth control was unacceptable. Today, they claim, the situation is very different.

Secondly there is divorce. Divorce is undoubtedly allowed in the Qur'an, yet Muslims perceived it as the last resort. Muhammad stated that it was something detestable. However, a man can divorce his wife by a public repudiation, then waiting three months to ensure that she is not pregnant by him. He can also repudiate her successively in each of the three months. Although it has given rise to abuse it is also possible for a man to divorce his wife by three repudiations without waiting the three months. A Muslim wife can also divorce her husband, however this is more difficult and requires a specific cause such as desertion, physical abuse or impotence.

Thirdly, the Qur'an allows women to inherit property. However, since in theory women are not burdened with financial care of families they may only inherit half of what male heirs receive in a particular inheritance.

For Westerners one of the most obvious features of the Muslim women is their dress. The veiling of Islamic women and their seclusion in harems has appealed significantly to Western imagination. The Qur'an made it clear that women should not be exposed to public view, but no specific instructions were given as to how this was to be accomplished. The wearing of a veil that covers part or all of the face and the wearing of the *chador* which covers the entire body seems to have developed as Islam came into contact with Byzantine Greek society in Syria, Iraq and Persia and was done to protect the women from strangers. Since the 1920s many Muslim women have sought liberation from these clothing regulations. At other times there has been a swing back the other way. The veil and the *chador* have been seen as a symbol of Islamic commitment and a repudiation of Western culture and values.

Islam today

Modern times have seen dramatic changes in Islam. The ideal of the religion has been to establish an Islamic world where all social processes are guided by the Pathway. In some Muslim countries societal institutions such as education, government and law are being de-Islamicised. Religion is becoming more a matter of personal preference rather than imposition. Side by side with this movement has been an Islamic resurgence, a quest for renewed commitment as a reaction to Western domination of the Arab peoples. The West is depicted as morally bankrupt, having exploited scientific and technical discoveries for its own purposes. Western political policies, Western economic policies, Western justice are all considered to be deficient. The response is the reinstatement of the Shariah as the true way of living.

> Islam is a complete code of life suitable for all people and all times, and Allah's mandate is eternal and universal and applies to every sphere of human conduct and life, without any distinction between the temporal and the spiritual.
>
> Universal Islamic Declaration, 1976

Both these trends will have consequences for the future development of Islamic ethics.

The Law of Allah and Muslim ethics are based on the

notion of a God who is the ordainer, whose will is law. Muslims must discover and formulate that will and carry it out in their lives. That is the basis of all Muslim moral practice. If a fundamental principle underlies Muslim ethics, comparable to covenant righteousness in Judaism or love in Christianity, then that principle is *islam*, submissiveness to Allah. The Pathway simply details the 'oughts' and the 'ought nots' of a way of life that has been totally surrendered to Allah.

4

Hinduism

Pronounced 'Orm' or 'Aum',
this is the most important
sound in Hinduism, the symbol
and expression of Brahman,
God. It is commonly used in
meditation and prayer.
Buddhists also use the sound.

Main dates of Hinduism

		BCE
Pre-Aryan Civilisation		2500
Aryan invasion from Central Asia	▼	2000
Age of Vedas		1000
Upanishads		800
Ideas of *karma*, rebirth, caste or *varna*		400
Code of Manu	▼	200
Mahabharata		
Bhagavad Gita		CE
Rise of *bhakti*		
Ramayana		200
Sankara, greatest of philosophers		800
Islam established in northern areas	▼	1000
Buddhism finally disappears from India		1300
Beginnings of Western impact	▼	1700
Rise of Hindu reform movements		1800
Mahatma Gandhi		1900
Independence: India becomes a secular state		1947

Set thy heart upon thy work but never on its reward.

Hinduism

The best known Hindu of modern times is without any doubt Mahatma Gandhi. His was a many-sided character: As the man who inspired the Indian nationalist movement from the early 1920s till his death in 1948 he had an enormous influence on the political life of his country. Yet he was utterly unlike most other political leaders both inside and outside India. His own followers were often puzzled by his leadership, and his opponents, the British, were mystified and exasperated by his tactics. Woven into Gandhi's campaign for his country's freedom were ideas and practices that came from India's dominant religious tradition, Hinduism. Self-government, for example, had to be won by *satygraha* or 'truth force' and the methods used against the British had to be in keeping with this concept. India's freedom fighters had to be people of *ahimsa* or 'harmlessness'. They had to be non-violent in their actions against the government; in their personal life they were expected to dress simply, to eat only vegetarian foods, to abstain from alcohol and, in general, to apply a strict discipline to themselves. Above all, while they might abhor British imperialism they were not to hate British officials.

The religious character of Gandhi's leadership was recognised by the masses throughout the country, and he became the *Mahatma* or 'great soul' of Hindu tradition. His life expressed the disciplined spirituality of Hinduism: he was a worshipper of Rama and Krishna, a supporter of caste, and a believer in the sacredness of the cow. At the same time he identified himself with India's untouchables, admired Jesus, valued political democracy as it was practised in Britain, and strove to see it implemented in a free and self-governing India. Gandhi was unquestionably a man of the spirit; he was also a shrewd political leader. He knew what he wanted for India—*swarajy* or 'self-government'—and he was determined to get it.

The combination of various qualities, attitudes and beliefs in the person of Mahatma Gandhi is typical of Hinduism. It is extremely difficult to define Hinduism, to say succinctly what constitutes the essence of this religion. It is a variegated phenomenon with many different aspects. Hinduism is best regarded as an umbrella-type word for the religious life which developed in India from about 2000 BCE. It covers the worship of gods and spirits of nature, the rituals associated with the changing seasons, the prayers and sacrifices offered to the many divine beings of Indian mythology and folk-lore, and the reflections of philosophers on the nature of human life and God. It also includes the system of social grouping known to Westerners by the term caste. Caste has meant that the mandatory social duties for people born into different groups have been very precisely defined. At the same time the teaching of Hindu philosophers has produced innumerable mystics, people who seek an ecstatic and transcendent salvation far beyond the world of everyday life with its mixture of duties and pleasures.

Basic ideas

Hinduism has always allowed its adherents a great deal of freedom in matters of belief. It has no founder whose words are regarded as the fountain of truth, it has no creed to which people are required to assent, and no pope or patriarch or imam to say what may or may not be taught. Nevertheless there are certain ideas which can be regarded

as basic to Hinduism because of their widespread acceptance in India.

The primary source of these ideas is a body of literature
known as the Upanishads. This word means 'sitting near
to' and evokes a common scene in Indian history, a *guru* or
'teacher' with a group of enquirers or disciples squatting in
front of him. The Upanishads consist of reflections of the
wise men of ancient India, from the period 800 to 400 BCE.
These gurus asked questions, probed into the meaning of
life rather than preaching a message from God. But time
has given their words a pre-eminent authority and the
Vedanta, the major philosophy based on the Upanishads,
has been studied and expounded by many generations of
Indian teachers. This philosophy has always had a practical side; it has been much more than a concern of intellec-
tuals. It has sought to give people an understanding of the
human situation in this life and, in keeping with its diagnosis of this condition, to give advice about a way of salvation or a method of human transformation.

The journeys of the soul

The first of the ideas coming from the Upanishads is that of
rebirth. We live and die and then we are born again, live
again and die again. The soul is caught up in *samsara*, 'the
cycle of life and death'. The many journeys of the soul into
life and, after death, into life again are not limited to the
level of human existence. The soul can be embodied in
animal as well as in human form.

> Those who are of good conduct here—the prospect is that they
> will come to a pleasant birth, either the birth of a priest, or the
> birth of a warrior, or the birth of a merchant. But those who are of
> evil conduct here—the prospect is that they will come to an evil
> birth, either the birth of a dog, or the birth of a swine, or the birth
> of an outcast.
>
> Chandogya Upanishad 5: 10

Law of karma

What we will be is determined by the way we live now. This is the law of *karma* or 'action' and it means quite simply that good actions will bear good fruit and bad actions bad fruit. We reap what we sow. We are what we are in this life because of the nature of our previous existence. All people, in fact all life, are reaping the fruit of their past. At the same time they are determining their destiny in their next existence.

These two ideas, rebirth and *karma*, clearly have ethical implications. High caste Hindus or wealthy Hindus can justify their privileged place in the social order by crediting the presumed quality of their previous lives. They can be proud, complacent and secure. They deserve to be what they are. Likewise, the appropriate attitude for low caste Hindus or persons living in poverty is passive acceptance of their lot. There is no injustice about the human condition; we are what the past has made us. All religions try to provide an answer to the problem of suffering, to why some people prosper and others endure pain and deprivation. The Hindu answer, because of *karma*, is that there is no problem. We are simply reaping our deserts, whatever form they may take.

There is little doubt that through the centuries these twin beliefs have helped many people accept the appalling conditions in which they have been forced to live. They have sanctioned the structures of Indian society such as caste and enabled people to live with some degree of serenity within their environment.

Karma can, of course, be looked at in another light. Not only is it an explanation of the present; it can also be seen as our opportunity to do something positive about the future. It is possible to live in this life so that the next embodiment of the soul will have a higher status and better life. Conditioned though we may be by past *karma* we nevertheless have some degree of freedom, and with that freedom we can determine what we *will* be. It is not surprising that this forward-looking view of *karma* is stressed by many modern Hindus. India is a developing country that looks towards the future rather than the past. Indians expect social improvement, wish to build a new India, and emphasise change; understandably this commitment to a new future for India's millions has an influence on the way the concept of *karma* is presented today.

Identity with God

The third idea from the Upanishads is that at the deepest level of our being we are one with God or, to use the Hindu word, Brahman. This is not a very easy idea for people in the West to grasp. Most of the time we are conscious of ourselves as distinct and separate individuals. We see ourselves as different from others and, because of the influence of the Jewish-Christian tradition, we also regard God as different and perhaps very remote from us. We speak of God as creator, lord and so on. In Indian religious philosophy, on the other hand, God is not separated from human beings. God pervades everything, and everyone. God, the World-Soul, is one and the same as the soul within us, which is the Divine Soul or *Atman*. Brahman and Atman are one and the same.

> He is my Self within the heart, smaller than a grain of rice, smaller than a grain of barley, smaller than a mustard seed, smaller than a grain of millet; He is my Self within the heart, greater than the earth, greater than the mid-region, greater than heaven, greater than all these worlds...He is my Self within the heart. He is that Brahman.
>
> Chandogya Upanishad 3: 14

The pursuit of salvation

We pass now to a fourth idea, that of *moksha*, 'liberation' or 'salvation'. The best way to approach this is to think of ourselves as living at two levels. At the lower level we live as individuals: we hope, we fear, we desire and we act. Each of us has a soul and that soul is subject to rebirth because of its actions. A person is enmeshed in a continuous cycle of births and rebirths. Salvation, according to Upanishadic tradition, is liberation from *samsara*, from this constant journeying of the soul from life to life. It is freedom from the sense of individuality which is our normal condition. Put another way, salvation is ascent out of the world of *karma* and rebirth to the highest plane of all, the mystical realisation of a person's essential divinity. Or it can be described as a transition from ignorance to knowledge, from a person's false view of self as an individual soul to the true knowledge that that person and God are one.

The way of knowledge

This knowledge, this mystical experience of divine-human oneness, has never been achieved, one imagines, by more than a handful of people throughout Indian history. And it has been a man's interest, a woman's religious life consisting of visits to the temple and the care of the shrine in the home honouring one or more of the gods. While there are varieties of belief in Hinduism it is generally understood that women cannot attain full salvation. They will have to await a better rebirth, which would normally mean being born again as a man. The ascetic way or life of extreme self-discipline involves yoga, literally the 'yoking' or control of a person's mental and physical processes and powers. This in itself places heavy demands on those who aspire to reach the goal; it also necessitates the rejection of values cherished by other people.

According to ancient Indian tradition there were four

stages in a man's life. As a young man he was expected to study, imbibing, under the guidance of a teacher, the wisdom of the ancient books known as the Vedas. In his second stage, he became a householder, raising a family and earning his living. In the third stage, somewhere around the age of forty-five, he was expected to withdraw from normal society, to study the Vedas, to practise yoga and to become less and less attracted by the pleasures of the material world. Finally, he became a *sanyasi*, one who renounced all worldly things and one whose constant concern was to meditate on the soul's union with God.

> Day after day, let the Yogi practise the harmony of soul in a secret place, in deep solitude, master of his mind, hoping for nothing, desiring nothing.
> Let him find a place that is pure and a seat that is restful, neither too high nor too low, with sacred grass and a skin and a cloth thereon.
> On that seat let him rest and practise Yoga for the purification of the soul; with the life of his body and mind in peace; his soul in silence before the One.
> With upright body, head, and neck, which rest still and move not; with inner gaze which is not restless, but rests still between the eye-brows;
> With soul in peace, and all fear gone, and strong in the vow of holiness, let him rest with mind in harmony, his soul on me, his God supreme.

Bhagavad Gita 6: 10–14*

If we ask about the ethical ideals implicit in such a view of salvation then the answer is that morality is subordinated to the quest for the transcendent spiritual experience. That which helps to prepare a man for knowledge of the eternal reality within him is right. Obviously this knowledge is not possible if a man is still aware of his duties to those around him. Ultimately, he has to renounce the world, as millions have done in India, and become a

---

*Quotations from the Bhagavad Gita in this chapter are from J. Mascaro (tr.), *Bhagavad Gita*, Penguin Classics, 1974.

wandering ascetic, attached to no place and to no group of people. He has to reject pleasure, to regard the world as ephemeral or of secondary importance and to conquer the desires that in previous stages of his life had made him a man of action. The morals of the yogi are the morals of a world-denying asceticism, of stern self-discipline for the sake of self-salvation.

Most Hindus, of course, have not been yogis and while the way of knowledge may be respected, it is not a road that many try to travel. It has less standing today than it had in the past. The modernisers of present-day India want a social morality that will help to transform society. The yogi and his example of withdrawal from community life are seen by many as irrelevant, a legacy from the past with nothing to contribute to the future.

The ordering of society

The sort of mysticism we have been describing is not concerned with the way society should be organised and governed. Such a mysticism has always been an integral part of Hinduism, but alongside this element and just as important is the support that Hinduism has given to the ordering of society. This is usually described as caste. For most Hindus social moral directives are very important indeed and concern what is required from them as members, by birth, of a particular caste.

There is a vast literature on caste and only the most important features can be mentioned here. It seems clear that from very early times Indian society was divided into four groups—the Brahmins or 'priests', the Kshatriyas or 'warriors', the Vaisyas or 'agriculturists and shopkeepers', and a servant class known as the Sudra. These four groups in the community were known as *varna*, a word meaning 'colour', and such a designation supports the generally accepted view that stratification began when the fair-skinned

Aryan invaders encountered the much darker indigenous inhabitants of north India (about 2000–1500 BCE). The characteristics expected from each *varna* were set out in the Code of Manu, the mythical progenitor of the human race. The importance of doing one's duty as a *varna* member is seen in this passage from the Bhagavad Gita.

> The works of Brahmins, Kshatriyas, Vaisyas and Sudras are different, in harmony with the three powers of their born nature.
> The works of a Brahmin are peace; self-harmony, austerity and purity; loving-forgiveness and righteousness; vision and wisdom and faith.
> These are the works of a Kshatriya; a heroic mind, inner fire, constancy, resourcefulness, courage in battle, generosity and noble leadership.
> Trade, agriculture and the rearing of cattle is the work of a Vaisya. And the work of the Sudra is service.
> They all attain perfection when they find joy in their work. Hear how a man attains perfection and finds joy in his work.
> A man attains perfection when his work is worship of God, from whom all things come and who is in all.
> Greater is thine own work, even if this be humble, than the work of another, even if this be great. When a man does the work God gives him, no sin can touch this man.
>
> Bhagavad Gita 18:41–7

It is doubtful whether social divisions were ever as clear-cut as the ancient books prescribe. Certainly as time went on the *varna* basis of society was transformed into a much more complex thing—the *jati* based divisions of Indian society (*jati* meaning 'birth'). The fourfold framework of classification gave way to a proliferation of sub-groups. Those of the same occupation formed a *jati* which gradually developed its own group customs. Furthermore some people, such as the scavengers, came to be regarded as spiritually polluted because of their occupation and so were despised as the *ashuddh*, the 'unclean', outcasts or untouchables. Many Hindus today (Gandhi was one) defend caste in its original *varna* form while rejecting caste as *jati* because of the social and religious apartheid associated with it. Certainly, they condemn untouchability as a complete perversion of the *varna* ideal. *Varna*, its defenders say, recognises the innate diversity among human beings while at the same time upholding the principle that society is an organic and comprehensive whole. The fact remains, however, that a four-class society is still a divided society, one in which a person's status and functions are fixed by birth; *karma* determines where and in what group a person will be born.

For those Indians determined to modernise their country, caste, both in its *varna* and *jati* forms, has to be eliminated. They see it as eventually succumbing to the influences of modern education, the growth of industries, the formation of new human groupings such as trade unions and political parties, and the emergence of a new Hinduism which will not provide a justification for caste as it has done in the past. The end of caste is a confident expectation; how long it will take for such an institution to wither and die only time will tell.

Duty: the way of works

The brief description of caste in the preceding section was a necessary prelude to a consideration of the *karma marg*, the 'way of works', by which millions in India have sought salvation. Hinduism has recognised that few people can walk the way of knowledge; for the majority the spiritual quest has to be undertaken within the given conditions of social life. Apart from salvation, the Hindu code laid down three goals that were legitimate for householders—*kama*, 'pleasure'; *artha*, 'economic success'; and *dharma*, 'duty'.

The first two illustrate another side of Hinduism, very different indeed from its philosophy and mysticism. Pleasure, including sexual enjoyment and prosperity, belongs very much to this world and to the state of individuality. Hinduism says that, in the stage of life as a householder, a person is justified in seeking satisfaction and enrichment of a physical or material kind.

The supremely important goal for the householder is *dharma* or duty. *Dharma* denotes a person's social responsibilities, what should be done because of the caste to which that person belongs. *Dharma* is binding; there is no escape from it and in the conditions of ordinary life it is the highest moral ideal. People must do their duty. In north India and in other Hindi speaking areas of India *dharma* has become synonymous with religion. The Christian religion for example is called the Christian *dharma*. It is the way of life that is an intrinsic feature of the Christian community, the moral and religious code that distinguishes the Christian group from other groups.

Dharma was often described in the writings of ancient India as a payment of debts. Certain things were due—a person owed to the gods the offering of sacrifice, to the gurus the study of the scriptures, and to the ancestors the procreation of children. In time it came to have a wider meaning. Duty today embraces both religious and social obligations. A person is expected to participate in caste ceremonies, to share in the group rituals connected with birth, marriage and death, and to worship in temples closely associated with one's caste. People are required to be loyal to their respective castes and to meet the demands that membership involves. The way of works is the way of *dharma*. The law books in their teaching about *dharma* also commended such virtues as truthfulness in the fulfilment of obligations to others.

This concept of *dharma* has tended to be limited in character and conservative in its effects. People certainly have extensive social responsibilities, according to traditional Hinduism, but they tend to be circumscribed by the walls of caste. There is little sense of a universal human community but a keen awareness of what the more proximate caste group requires. By insisting on the importance of social duty, defined in caste terms, conservatism is encouraged. Whatever is best, what the ancestors did in days gone by, the children must do now. Some modern Hindus are reminting the idea of *dharma*, and the main stimulus for this change is the nationalism that has developed in the last hundred years. The concept, it is now said, has to be released from its bondage to caste and applied to the life of the wider community and to that of the nation and the world. For such Indians duty to the nation and, ideally, to humanity, is an example of the way a very ancient idea can be reinterpreted.

Duty and the love of God

As well as the ways of knowledge and works, there is a third way of salvation in Hinduism, *bhakti marg* or 'the way of devotion'. In this way, *dharma* remains paramount; we must do our duty but the spirit in which we do so must be one of selflessness. Our actions must be infused with the love of God. But what is meant by 'God'?

Indians regard religion as a quest, in which human beings reach out beyond themselves towards that which is ultimate. In their ardour they may fix their affections upon a multiplicity of supernatural beings. Devotees make use of the gods, who might be nature deities or heroes from Hindu mythology, in order to seek both peace and power from a reality that is beyond human description. Which god they choose is up to them and their spiritual preference and capacity. Religions differ, the gods differ because people differ. Belief in many gods is a reflection of the wide diversity of spirituality that characterises humankind. According to Hindu belief, any god is true if it is true for someone's spiritual need.

This approach to the question of religious truth makes Hinduism a most hospitable religion. No god can be excluded from the Hindu pantheon and people should not say that their god, their way of worship, is the only way. Writers on Hinduism stress its religious tolerance. This quality is certainly present in its accommodating attitude towards polytheism in belief and worship. It is far less evident in social behaviour where, for example, a person who converts to Christianity and thereby rejects caste may be the victim of intolerant persecution.

One of the most important and influential of the Hindu writings is the little volume known as the Gita, or, in its full title, Bhagavad Gita, the Song of the Blessed One. This anonymous work, written probably two thousand years ago, is today a source of great inspiration to Hindus. Over the centuries people have written and continue to write expositions of its message. It had a great influence on Gandhi. Its status is sometimes likened to that which many Christians give to the Sermon on the Mount, which they regard as containing the essence of Jesus' teaching. The Gita illustrates the comprehensiveness of Hinduism in that it unites the quest for Brahman with fervent devotion to a particular god, in this case Krishna.

The Gita is important for our purpose because of the way a number of passages set morality in the context of the love of God (conceived as Krishna). In order to see this, some background information is necessary. The Gita is part of a much larger work, the epic called the Mahabharata. This purports to be the account, a very long one, of a conflict between related clans of Kshatriyas or warriors. Arjuna is the leader of one of the warring families and Krishna is the driver of his chariot. Arjuna becomes affected by the bloodshed and by the fact that he is being forced to kill his cousins. In his anguish he appeals to Krishna for guidance. The dialogue that ensues constitutes the content of the Gita. The answers given by Krishna, who in the course of the poem is transformed from a charioteer into a divine being, extol the virtue of duty while indicating the spirit in which that duty should be performed.

The *dharma* or duty of the Kshatriya was to fight and that carried with it, of course, the inevitability of death for some of the warriors. Is there any alternative to fighting and killing? For the warrior, Krishna's answer is *no*. If Arjuna refused to fight he would tarnish his honour as a member of the fighting caste; he must do the work, the *dharma*, that destiny has given him. Krishna does, however, console Arjuna by pointing out that there resides within each person the eternal reality or Brahman. Death may destroy individual bodies, but it does not touch the real person, the divine which abides beneath the superficial expressions of individuality.

> Interwoven in his creation, the Spirit is beyond destruction. No one can bring to an end the Spirit which is everlasting.
>
> For beyond time he dwells in these bodies, though these bodies have an end in their time; but he remains immeasurable, immortal.
>
> Therefore, great warrior, carry on thy fight.
>
> If any man thinks he slays, and if another thinks he is slain, neither knows the ways of truth. The Eternal in man cannot kill; the Eternal in man cannot die.
>
> He is never born, and he never dies. He is in Eternity; he is for evermore. Never-born and eternal, beyond times gone or to come, he does not die when the body dies.
>
> Weapons cannot hurt the Spirit and fire can never burn him. Untouched is he by drenching waters, untouched is he by parching winds.
>
> Beyond the power of sword and fire, beyond the power of waters and winds, the Spirit is everlasting, omnipresent, never-changing, never-moving, ever One.
>
> Bhagavad Gita 2: 17–20, 23–4

This may not be much comfort to the soldier being killed; he is after all, more conscious of his individual being than of the divine spirit within him. Pain is certainly real to those who live with little or no knowledge of the presence in each person of an inviolable divine essence.

Krishna is quite emphatic about the duty of a warrior, and what he says about one caste is implied for all. The ethical message of the Gita upholds the roles and responsibility assigned to every person by virtue of birth into a caste. The Gita recognises also that salvation is possible in the everyday world of action. This somewhat different interpretation of the way of works has two important features.

The first is that people should act, they should do their *dharma*, in a spirit of detachment as far as reward or punishment in a future rebirth is concerned. They should strive to free themselves from any expectation about whether they will benefit or suffer from what they are doing. Actions performed with desire for a reward, duty done in a spirit of self-interest—this will simply keep them in the cycle of life and rebirth. To act disinterestedly, without hope or fear, is a higher form of action. It is the way of wisdom.

Set thy heart upon thy work, but never on its reward. Work not for a reward; but never cease to do thy work.

Do thy work in the peace of Yoga and, free from selfish desires, be not moved in success or in failure. Yoga is evenness of mind—a peace that is ever the same.

Work done for a reward is much lower than work done in the Yoga of wisdom.

He who withdraws himself from actions, but ponders on their pleasures in his heart, he is under a delusion and is a false follower of the Path.

But great is the man who, free from attachments, and with a mind ruling its powers in harmony, works on the path of Karma Yoga, the path of consecrated action.

Action is greater than inaction; perform therefore thy task in life. Even the life of the body could not be if there were no action.

Bhagavad Gita 2: 47–9, 3: 6–8

The second feature of this path, as expounded in the Gita, is that disinterested work is possible to those who set their affections on a personal god. In the Gita this is, of course, Krishna. (Indian devotion is not exclusive, however, and a person may find inspiration in Rama, Siva or a host of other deities.) God, as a focus of love, becomes the one for whom duty is done, the divine beloved for whose sake all actions are performed. Passages in the Gita illustrate this fusion of *dharma* and *bhakti*, of duty and devotion, inculcating the love of God as the highest motivation of behaviour.

> But they for whom I am the End Supreme, who surrender all their works for me, and who with pure love meditate on me and adore me—these I very soon deliver from the ocean of death and life-in-death, because they have set their heart on me.

> Set thy heart on me alone, and give to me thy understanding; thou shalt in truth live in me hereafter.

> If thou art not able to practise concentration, consecrate all thy work to me. By merely doing actions in my service thou shalt attain perfection.

> And if even this thou art not able to do, then take refuge in devotion to me and surrender to me the fruit of all thy work—with the selfless devotion of a humble heart.

> For concentration is better than mere practice, and meditation is better than concentration; but higher than meditation is surrender in love of the fruit of one's actions, for on surrender follows peace.

> Offer to me all thy works and rest thy mind on the Supreme. Be free from vain hopes and selfish thoughts, and with inner peace fight thou thy fight.

> Those who ever follow my doctrine and who have faith, and have a good will, find through pure work their freedom.

> Offer in thy heart all thy works to me, and see me as the End of thy love, take refuge in the Yoga of reason, and ever rest thy soul in me.

If thy soul finds rest in me, thou shalt overcome all dangers by my grace, but if thy thoughts are on thyself, and thou wilt not listen, thou shalt perish.

Bhagavad Gita 12: 6–8, 10–12; 3: 30–1; 18: 57–8

Bhakti, the love of God in some form, has undoubtedly affected the piety of the vast majority of Hindus. In the Gita the Supreme is manifested as Krishna; in the other great epic, the Ramayana, it is Rama, and in other writings other conceptions of deity receive devotion.

Some current issues

The Constitution of India, adopted after independence in 1947, made the country a secular state; that is, no religion was recognised as official and freedom was guaranteed to all religious groups. The vast majority of the Indian people are Hindus, professing a great variety of beliefs. In the absence of a unifying religious organisation led by recognised leaders, the state of India is free of the sort of coercive influence from religious personalities that we have seen in recent years in Muslim Iran. The idea of a Hindu state does, however, have its adherents and some political parties have an ideology that favours the protection and preservation of Hindu interests. This policy runs the risk of alienating followers of other religions, especially Islam. Communalism, as it is called, the stress on membership in one's own religious community and antipathy towards those belonging to other groups, has for decades caused division, and sometimes violence, in India. The best defence against it is the privatisation of religion and the upholding in public life of the liberal and democratic values, largely imbibed from the British, that were espoused by those who drew up the Constitution.

As far as bio-ethical issues are concerned, there is nowhere near the amount of debate in India that now takes place in many Western countries. Much more important is the provision of basic services to the many millions of Indians, especially in the villages, who are deprived of the advantages of modern medicine. Many still believe that disease may be caused by evil demons. Alongside the growth of modern or international medicine, India still has practitioners of *Ayurveda*, a collection of medical lore that makes use of natural remedies. This goes back over two thousand years and there is evidence that dispensaries providing medical services to the poor existed in ancient India, often associated with temples. Largely because of the influence of such ideas as *karma* and rebirth, and the esteem in which large families are held, Hindus tend to be generally conservative in medical matters. This outlook is changing as new ideas exert their influence.

Hindu attitudes towards the environment

India is a developing country and the need for economic growth, as much as possible and as fast as possible, affects the stance taken towards the environment. People may be concerned about ecology but it tends to take second place to economic interests. The traditional Hindu attitude to the world is that the entire creation can be seen as pervaded by God. Certain parts (rivers, mountains, trees for example) can acquire a special status in Hindu mythology and be regarded as 'sacred'. God is not transcendent, standing separate and apart from the world; rather his being flows through all creation. There is a sort of hierarchy in creation with the human being at the apex because of the capacity to realise unity with God. Another strand in Hinduism—as we saw in dealing with the way of knowledge—puts so much stress on this mystical union that the world is treated as unimportant, even illusory.

Women in Hinduism

Religious leadership in Hinduism has been largely a male affair. It was Brahmin men who read the Vedas, recited the sacred texts, performed the rituals, and walked the ascetic path in the quest of liberating knowledge. The women's way was that of *bhakti*, devotion to the gods worshipped in the home or in public shrines. For many the model of a devoted wife was provided by one of the goddesses, especially Sita, the loyal, chaste, docile and humble consort of Rama. When British rule began to be influential from the early nineteenth century there was a great deal of Western concern regarding the place of women in Hindu society, especially sati (the immolation of a wife on the funeral pyre of her husband), child marriage, female infanticide and the treatment of widows. Reformers, both Hindu and Western, were responsible for the abolition of sati (1829), the legalisation of widow remarriage (1856) and the introduction of education for girls. Since then there have been changes, most influential in the middle and upper classes, that have resulted in many women taking part in professional and political life. In a country with a population as large as that of India and with entrenched centuries-old attitudes it has to be said that a new outlook in male-female relationships has yet to affect the masses of people.

Conclusion

Hinduism has been throughout Indian history a many-sided religious movement, but it has given a high degree of unity to the cultural life of the sub-continent. It has provided clear ethical guidance for groups within its social system; it has given men and women gods to love and to sing about. Today Hinduism is changing and facing challenges as it encounters ideological and religious concepts that press upon it from the outside world. Ethically, it is subject to extreme pressure. Hinduism has always been ready to absorb ideas that were not present in its ancient literature. It is an ever-growing and changing movement and Hindu ethics will respond to new challenges. Perhaps in fifty years or less *dharma*—the heart of Hindu morality—will mean something vastly different from what it has in the past.

5
Buddhism

The wheel is a common
Buddhist symbol for Buddha's
teaching. His first sermon 'set
in motion the wheel of the
Doctrine'. The wheel is used in
some cultures as a symbol of
the sun, eternity and of the
cycle of life.

Main dates of Buddhism

	BCE
Birth of Buddha	563
Buddhism spreads in north India	300
Buddhism spreads to Sri Lanka	
then to Thailand and Burma	
Asoka, Indian king, becomes Buddhist	200
	CE
Mahayana Buddhism begins	100
Buddhism spreads to China	200
Buddhism enters Japan	600
Tibetan Buddhism develops	
Chinese and Japanese sects emerge	
Japanese Buddhist preacher, Nichiren	1300
Growth of Zen and other sects	
Buddhism spreads to the West;	
societies formed in Europe and the USA	1900
Sixth Buddhist World Council,	
Rangoon	1954

Better than a thousand useless words is one single word that gives peace.

Buddhism

The birth of Buddhism can be dated. Unlike Hinduism, Buddhism had a founder, Gautama, the person history knows as the Buddha. The religion called Buddhism arose out of his personal understanding of the meaning of life. The date often given for his birth is 563 BCE and for his death 483 BCE. Eventually this faith, which was first expounded in the towns and cities of north India, all but disappeared from the land of its birth. But outside India, it spread with remarkable vigour.

Buddhism today is the major faith of Sri Lanka (Ceylon), Burma, Thailand, Laos, Cambodia and Vietnam. For centuries it was one of the ingredients in Chinese religion. A similar syncretism or intermingling of religious ideas has characterised the relationship between Buddhism and Shintoism in Japan. The wide spread and long history of this religion, in so many different cultures, inevitably resulted in a variety of forms of Buddhism. There is no one Buddhism. Buddhist sects abound and some, especially in Japan, contend that their interpretation of the Buddha's teaching is the right one. Even where sects have not proliferated, the main stream of Buddhist teaching has merged with religions that prevailed in the area before Buddhism.

The terms used for the major divisions of Buddhism are Theravada and Mahayana. Theravada, 'the teaching of the elders', is sometimes called Hinayana, 'the lesser vehicle'. It claims to embody most faithfully the teaching of

Gautama and the first leaders of the movement. It takes as normative three collections of ancient scriptures known as the *Tripitika* or 'three baskets'. These were declared authoritative at councils of monks held in the first two centuries after the death of Buddha. Theravada is practised in such southern Asian countries as Sri Lanka, Burma and Thailand; as a result some writers call it Southern Buddhism.

Mahayana means 'great vehicle' (of salvation) and the use of such a term highlights the fact that, in the first few centuries of the Common Era, a form of Buddhism developed in north India which regarded itself as superior to Theravada. It claimed to be the *great* vehicle, offering people a salvation that was considered more sure, more accessible, more satisfying and more comprehensive than that offered by followers of Theravada. The latter was dismissed as Hinayana, 'the lesser or small vehicle'; it was 'small' because only a few could expect to persevere in the life of demanding discipline that led to salvation. Although it originated in India, the main influence of Mahayana has always been north and east of the Himalayas. It has been a far less homogeneous movement than Theravada, spawning dozens of sects (in Japan it is still doing so), and most scholars agree that some of the differences between Mahayana and Theravada are so great as to be irreconcilable.

In this chapter we will deal, firstly, with the ethical system of Theravada. Then the main Mahayana deviations will be outlined.

Buddha and his truths

Buddha (for that is how we shall now speak of him) grew up in Hindu India where people worshipped the gods, believed in the law of *karma* and rebirth, and where sages were concerned with salvation from *samsara*, the cycle of life and death. Like many others he became interested in the way of knowledge, the search for salvation. He became an ascetic, wandering from place to place, listening to those who talked of the highest of the Hindu ways and wondering if this was indeed true knowledge. He spent six years, according to the traditional account, in a life of unrelenting self-denial. But the sense of peace, a concomitant of salvation, still eluded him. Thoroughly debilitated in health, depressed in spirit and beset by temptations, he rested under a tree near the modern city of Gaya in the northern state of Bihar. There, as he meditated, something happened to him. For Buddhists the experience was without question one of enlightenment, the light of wisdom, *bodhi*, shone within him. He saw why life was so full of suffering, what caused rebirth and how people could be liberated from the twin forces of *karma* and *samsara*. He became the enlightened one, the Buddha.

From that time onwards, Buddha saw himself as the bearer of a message, the teacher of the *dharma* or doctrine that could transform people's lives. He spent the remainder of a very long life sharing with others his concept of what life could become. In Buddhist parlance he set in motion and kept turning 'the wheel of the Doctrine'. The core of this doctrine is contained in the Four Noble Truths.

The first of these is that life is suffering. Buddha began with the simple affirmation that human existence is characterised by pain, impermanence and dissatisfaction. This may seem a very doleful view of life, but for Buddhism it is an honest recognition of what life is really like. Nothing can satisfy us, always or fully. Pleasure gives way to pain, youth to age, health to sickness and life to death. Everything with which we deal in this life, including our own being, is subject to constant change. The first step to wisdom is to see how incomplete and painful life is.

The second truth is that the suffering of life is due to craving, desire or thirst. Craving for what? The Buddhist answer is that people strive to establish themselves at the centre of their world, they try to enhance their own egos which, quite wrongly, seem to be of supreme importance. They crave power, security, material possessions. They want to go on living and at the end they want rebirth in a future existence. They become victims of what are called the three intoxications—the sensuality that makes them love the pleasures of this world, the ignorance that deludes them into holding wrong views about themselves, and the craving that makes them long for rebirth.

The third truth is that craving must be extinguished. But how can this be done?

The answer is set out in Buddha's fourth truth; the seeker after salvation must walk the Noble Eightfold Path. The steps that must be taken are as follows:

Right belief *Right purpose*	These involve the acceptance of the first three truths and the determination to effect a change.
Right speech e.g. avoidance of anger, gossip and boasting *Right conduct* e.g. acts of kindness, avoidance of quarrelling *Right livelihood* e.g. living according to Buddhist principles	These are basic moral requirements amplified later in the rules for monks and the virtues commended for lay people.
Right effort *Right mind control* *Right meditation*	These refer to the life of meditation, usually in a monastery.

The image of a path carries with it that of a destination. The Path leads somewhere; those who travel on it are seeking a goal. That goal, Buddhist salvation, is the experience of nirvana, the extinction of individuality and desires. A person who reaches this end becomes an *Arahat* or, as it is usually put in English, a saint. People who attain this goal become new beings, liberated from all the fetters that bound them to a life of ignorance and immune to all intoxications that stimulated their craving. Desire has no more domination over them, the world has lost its seductive power—they are free, free from craving in this life and free from craving for rebirth.

The doctrine and the way

We are now in a position to describe in greater detail the morality that emanated from the doctrine or body of ideas propounded by Buddha. Buddhist ethics in their pristine form were a philosophy of life, a view of humankind and the world. The major ethical tradition in Hinduism, as we saw in the last chapter, is concerned with maintaining the structures of society, with the inculcation of a strong sense of social duty. Buddhist morality is much more personal; it is the way of life for those who want to reach nirvana. There is a major difference between the Hindu concept of *dharma* as duty and the Buddhist use of the word. (This is normally written in the Pali scriptures of Buddhism as *dhamma.*) Buddhism sees dharma as a universal truth about all human life. Dharma insists that human life is essentially a suffering or non-fulfilled existence, that change and impermanence are universal, that human beings have a deep-seated craving within them. From this inward craving results rebirth. This is how life is. Until people know or are grasped by this truth about themselves, they dwell not in light but in darkness. The Eightfold Path and its later expansion have to be placed firmly within the context of a set

137

of beliefs which, for Buddhists, have the ring of truth or ultimacy about them.

So far, nothing has been said about God and what Buddha taught about the divine. Tradition has it that he refused to indulge in speculation about the origin of the world and about how any ultimate reality or God should be described. The Four Truths stand, for the Buddhist, on their own merits as a diagnosis of the human condition and a prescription for utterly transforming that unhappy state of affairs. They are accepted as true, partly because it is believed that those who act upon them discover in their own experience that they are true; they do give salvation, they do lead to nirvana.

Even in strongly Theravada countries such as Thailand, people still make offerings at the shrines of many spirits and gods. These practices illustrate the ease with which Buddhism can merge with pre-Buddhist or non-Buddhist beliefs. The orthodox Theravadin regards the gods (and all beings in any other realms beyond our comprehension) as being subject, like human beings, to impermanence and change. Animism or spirit-worship, it is argued, is only concerned with worldly needs. A person asks the spirits and gods for a good harvest, for good health, prosperity and so on. Spirit or god-religion has nothing to do with the realisation of nirvana; for guidance and direction in this quest a person has to go to one source, Buddha.

It will be apparent that Buddhist morality consists of the observance of those principles and precepts that will ultimately result in the conquest of craving and the attainment of salvation. Morality is a means to the realisation of a transcendent experience. The way of life set forth in the literature of Theravada is also a morality totally devoid of supernatural support and sanction. There is no promise of divine grace or aid to make the task easier. We must save ourselves; how far we travel along the Path to nirvana depends on our own steadfast perseverance. The Buddhist morality is an expression of Buddhist humanism. Buddha himself is reported as saying:

> Be ye lamps unto yourselves. Rely on yourselves, and do not rely on external help.
> Hold fast to the truth as a lamp. Seek salvation alone in the truth. Look not for assistance to anyone besides yourselves.

E. A. Burtt (ed.), *The Teachings of the Compassionate Buddha*, New American Library, New York, 1955.

Similar words are found in the Dhammapada, a collection of sayings or proverbs that have been part of the devotional currency of Buddhists in South-East Asia for two thousand years:

> Arise! Rouse thyself by thy Self; train thyself by thy Self. Under the shelter of thy Self, and ever watchful, thou shalt live in supreme joy.
> For thy Self is the master of thyself, and thy Self is thy refuge. Train therefore thyself well, even as a merchant trains a fine horse.
> In a fullness of delight and of faith in the teaching of Buddha, the mendicant monk finds peace supreme and beyond the transience of time, he will find the joy of Eternity, the joy supreme of Nirvana.

Dhammapada 379–81*

Some features of religious morality associated with Judaism and Christianity have no place within the framework of Buddhism. Sin and guilt are absent from the Buddhist analysis of the human condition. Many Christians would define sin as an offence against God's will or God's law, and guilt as the estrangement that results from this disobedience. The Buddhist does not talk this way. Buddhists consider a person's state, however undesirable, as a result of past *karma*, of actions in a previous life, and continued ignorance of the doctrine. We do not need forgiveness and there is no God who dispenses it. What we need is the enlightenment of Buddha's teaching and the resolve to act upon it.

*Quotations are taken from J. Mascaro (tr.), *The Dhammapada*, Penguin Classics, 1974.

The way of life required by the doctrines was first demonstrated by Buddha himself. The oldest summary of the Buddhist way, the *Triratna* or 'Three Jewels', begins 'I take refuge in the Buddha'. The other two affirmations are 'I take refuge in the doctrine' and 'I take refuge in the *sangha* or monastic society'. This chapter shows why the doctrine is indeed a 'jewel', a thing of value to Buddhists. The Buddha, the Buddhist teaching and the monastic society offer Buddhists the ability to find ultimate meaning in life.

What does it mean to take refuge in Buddha? What contribution does he make to the moral endeavours of the Buddhist?

Buddha is both the teacher and exemplar of truth. For Buddhists he shows the way. Orthodox Buddhists in South-East Asia stress the humanity of Buddha; it is extremely important. What he did others can do; it was as a human being that he found enlightenment, and in theory at least, other people have just as much chance of being successful. It is often thought that Buddhists worship or say prayers to Buddha, and the proliferation of Buddha-images is good ground for this belief. No doubt many Buddhists do believe that Buddha is now a supernatural being who can help them or that a Buddha-image has a peculiar power upon which they can draw. Strict Theravadins regard such beliefs as an adulteration of the pure doctrine. For them Buddha is 'dead' as far as petitionary prayer is concerned.

On his earthly demise he entered nirvana and nirvana is not a heavenly place from which he or any other liberated saint can exert an influence on conditions in this earthly realm. Buddha is a saviour only in the sense that he showed humankind the way and described the truths upon which that way is based. The function of Buddha-images is to assist those who are engaged in meditation; they are aids to reflection, not objects of worship.

The morality of the monk

The third refuge of the Buddhist is the *sangha* or society of monks. The founding of the monastic order or society is attributed to Buddha himself, membership being open to all those, irrespective of caste, who accepted the doctrine and wanted to follow the Eightfold Path. It is believed that in the beginning Buddha founded an order for women as well as for men. The Eightfold Path was open to both sexes and the attainment of nirvana was a goal for, all, even though some early texts make it clear that the primary responsibility for teaching the doctrine lay with the male *sangha*.

The order is not an optional extra in Buddhism; it is an essential part of the doctrine. If a person undertakes the serious and sustained search for nirvana he or she must withdraw into an environment where prolonged meditation is possible and where there are none of the distractions of normal social life. The moral life, implicit in the doctrine, is a means to salvation and that life (or the advanced stages of it) can only be fully undertaken within the discipline and with the support of the *sangha*.

Buddha reputedly laid down Ten Precepts or rules for members of the order. They explicate what was stated in the Eightfold Path. A monk has to promise:

Not to destroy life
Not to steal
Not to engage in sexual misconduct
Not to lie
Not to drink alcoholic beverages
Not to eat after midday
Not to take part in amusements such as dancing, singing and the theatre
Not to wear ornaments, use perfumes or dress extravagantly
Not to sleep on comfortable beds
Not to accept money

As time went on further rules became necessary. The result was a compilation known as the *Patimokha*. This consists of 227 rules, a catalogue of standards by which monks should judge themselves, and of perils which they should avoid. The list is recited by monks twice each lunar month.

The purpose behind the monks' morality is the ultimate extinction of craving. The monk is to live simply, to avoid luxury, and to be a centre of serenity rather than turbulence in the community. Constant meditation results in total self-control.

> Good is the control of the eye, and good is the control of the ear; good is the control of smell, and good is the control of taste.
> Good is the control of the body, and good is the control of words; good is the control of the mind, and good is the control of our whole inner life. When a monk has achieved perfect self-control, he leaves all sorrows behind.

Dhammapada 360-1

Liberation from all that stimulates craving means that a monk is on the way to nirvana.

> The monk who is full of love and who fully lives in the law of Buddha, he follows the path of Nirvana, the path of the end of all sorrow, the path of infinite joy.
> Empty the boat of your life, O man; when empty it will swiftly sail. When empty of passions and harmful desires you are bound for the land of Nirvana.
> Cut off the five—selfishness, doubt, wrong austerities and rites, lust, hate; throw off the five—desire to be born with a body, or without a body, self-will, restlessness, ignorance; but cherish five—faith, watchfulness, energy, contemplation, vision. He who has broken the five fetters—lust, hate, delusion, pride, false views—is one who has crossed to the other shore.
> But he who enjoys peaceful thoughts, who considers the sorrows of pleasure, and who ever remembers the light of his life—he will break the chains of death.
> He has reached the end of his journey, he trembles not, his cravings are gone, he is free from sin, he has burnt the thorns of life; this is his last mortal body.
> He is free from lust, he is free from greed, he knows the meaning of words, and the meaning of their combinations, he is a great man, a great man who sees the Light; this is his last mortal body.

Dhammapada 368–70, 350–2

Most of the admonitions regarding behaviour in early Buddhist literature are quite explicitly addressed to monks following the system of self-discipline that will result in enlightenment and the ineffable experience of nirvana. This does not mean, however, that Buddhism has no message for ordinary people, for those who for some reason or other do not take the yellow robe and enter a monastery. The morality of the laity will be dealt with in the next section. First we will examine the *sangha* and its place in the wider Buddhist society.

The order lives within and on the basis of a supporting Buddhist community. The monks receive their daily food from the laity. In theory they are not beggars; they give lay people the opportunity to acquire merit or to improve their spiritual standing by their gifts. Furthermore, it is quite common in South-East Asia for lay people themselves to spend some time within a monastery. Where tradition still reigns, young men, as part of their transition to adulthood, go for some weeks into the monastic society. Many people do so each year during the rainy season. Monks may also at any time withdraw from the order and resume secular occupations. The respect in which monks are held in traditional communities and their close association with lay people have meant that the order has been a leaven in Buddhist populations. The *sangha* has been a moral and spiritual light and its beams have reached far beyond the walls of its monasteries.

The Buddhist *sangha* has little or no heritage of social or political activism; it has not been a reformist movement. How could it be when its main purpose was to provide the setting in which a monk reached the blissful condition of being unaffected by both the world's pain and the world's pleasure? In recent years the non-political character of the *sangha* has been affected by nationalist sentiment and modern education so that in Burma in the 1930s and in Ceylon (now Sri Lanka) in the 1950s, the order exerted considerable political pressure over the issues of the time. In Burma Buddhist monks supported the movement for independence from the British; in Ceylon they opposed the dominance of a Westernised Christian élite in Ceylon's politics and education. In other less spectacular ways modern ideas are now modifying the nature of the Buddhist order. Its many schools in Thailand are now teaching more secular subjects than in the past, and monks are sharing in programmes of social change in towns and villages. They are the natural leaders, especially in rural areas, and their influence, and that of the order, are likely to remain significant for many years to come.

The virtues of the laity

Lay people in Theravada Buddhism are expected to support the monks in their quest. This support may take many forms, from the daily offering of food, to the building and upkeep of monasteries. The laity of course are still subject to craving and ignorance. So they marry, bring up their children, run their farms, carry on trade and remain active in the affairs of the world. In a community where everybody is a Buddhist, exposure to the monastic order means, however, that certain practices and virtues are encouraged among ordinary Buddhists while counsel is given about the vices that should be avoided.

Buddha taught that the first five of the Ten Precepts are obligatory for lay people. They should also treasure the *Triratna* or 'three jewels'—the Buddha, the doctrine and the order—and be receptive to the teaching of the monks. For lay Buddhists the virtues are friendliness, compassion, joy and equanimity.

Metta or 'friendliness, benevolence or love' is an important Buddhist virtue. It is the moral ideal to which people should aspire in their personal relationships, and it is all-embracing in its scope.

144

As a mother cares for her son,
Her only son, all her days,
So towards all things living
A man's mind should be all-embracing.
Friendliness for the whole world,
All-embracing, he should raise in his
mind,
Above, below, and across,
Unhindered, free from hate and ill-will.

Sutta Nipata

Metta means that people avoid quarrelling, control their temper and strive always for peace. Here are three extracts from the Dhammapada:

What we are today comes from our thoughts of yesterday, and our present thoughts build our life of tomorrow; our life is the creation of our mind.

If a man speaks or acts with a pure mind, joy follows him as his own shadow.

'He insulted me, he hurt me, he defeated me, he robbed me.' Those who think such thoughts will not be free from hate.

For hate is not conquered by hate; hate is conquered by love. This is a law eternal.

Many do not know that we are here in this world to live in harmony. Those who know this do not fight against each other.

Better than a thousand useless words is one single word that gives peace.

Better than a thousand useless verses is one single verse that gives peace.

Better than a hundred useless poems is one single poem that gives peace.

If a man should conquer in battle a thousand and a thousand more, and another man should conquer himself, his would be the greater victory, because the greatest of victories is the victory over oneself; and neither the gods in heaven above nor the demons down below can turn into defeat the victory of such a man.

Forsake anger, give up pride. Sorrow cannot touch the man who is not in the bondage of anything, who owns nothing.

145

> He who can control his rising anger as a coachman controls his carriage at full speed, this man I call a good driver; others merely hold the reins.
>
> Overcome anger by peacefulness, overcome evil by good. Overcome the mean by generosity, and the man who lies by truth.
>
> Dhammapada 2–6, 100–5, 221–3

The figure of the ideal man stands out clearly in the writings of Buddhism and Buddhism would refer specifically to an 'ideal man' rather than an 'ideal woman'. He is not an activist, a righter of wrongs, a campaigner for a new world. Rather, he is a man of peace, content with what life calls upon him to do or to bear, sustained by an inner joy and a serenity that is not dispelled by disaster or success. That this ideal has not always been realised goes without saying. A man must, therefore, be on his guard against a range of vices of which this extract gives a sample.

> What are the four vices of action that he gives up? They are injury to life, taking what is not given, base conduct in sexual matters, and false speech...
>
> What are the four motives of evil deeds which he avoids? Evil deeds are committed from partiality, enmity, stupidity, and fear.
>
> And what are the six ways of squandering wealth? They are addiction to drink, the cause of carelessness; roaming the streets at improper times; frequenting fairs; gambling; keeping bad company; and idleness.
>
> There are six dangers in addition to drink; actual loss of wealth, increased liability to quarrels; liability to illness; loss of reputation; indecent exposure; and weakened intelligence.
>
> Admonition to Singala

What does the lay Buddhist expect to reap from the cultivation of a life of virtue? The answer to this question takes us back to the ideas of *karma* and rebirth. Living according to the doctrine will not bring the lay person to nirvana. Only those who join the order and accept the discipline it prescribes can hope to reach that goal. People can, however, contribute towards their eventual salvation. By their good deeds they are ensuring that *karma* will give them a good rebirth, possibly with spiritual capacities that will enable them to take all the steps along the Eightfold Path.

The virtues that we have been describing in this section are not the only means open to the person who wants to build up a good credit balance, as it were, in the bank of *karma*. A person can also do this by performing acts of merit. Merit plays a very important part in the life of the Buddhist. Pious lay people stress a variety of actions that contribute towards the devotee's good *karma*. To respect monks and respond to their needs makes much merit.

> Weeds harm the fields, passions harm human nature; offerings given to those free from passions bring a great reward.
>
> Weeds harm the fields, hate harms human nature; offerings given to those free from hate bring a great reward.
>
> Weeds harm the fields, illusion harms human nature; offerings given to those free from illusion bring a great reward.
>
> Weeds harm the fields, desire harms human nature; offerings given to those free from desire bring a great reward.
>
> Dhammapada 356-9

Examples of other acts of merit are the building of pagodas, the decoration of temples and images of Buddha, benefactions to monasteries, meditation before an image, pilgrimages to sacred places, and the giving of alms to the poor. The religious idea of merit in a number of South-East Asian countries has considerable social and economic importance. It enhances the status and wealth of the *sangha* and sometimes results in lavish expenditure on religious objects.

Like all Asian religions Theravada is now exposed to the values inherent in modernisation. The quality and nature of the exposure varies. Bangkok is subjected to influences which so far have barely touched many villages in Thailand. Urbanisation and industry, the concern with national defence, internal conflict, ideologies such as Marxism, the growth of non-religious education, the orientation of monks towards a positive this-worldly service to the laity, the social problems resulting from tourism, and the influence of Western concepts of society are among the pressures impinging on traditional Theravada Buddhism. There is no doubt that it will change. But it will probably continue to be for a long time yet what it has been for centuries: the framework for the understanding of life and the source of virtue for millions of people in South and South-East Asia.

Mahayana and its saviours

The evolution of Mahayana as a distinct form of Buddhism began in north-western India about two thousand years ago. It later developed in quite different cultural and religious environments from those that existed in Theravada areas. In China, Mahayana's ideas of the divine were affected by the popular religion, Taoism, and its ethical influence was always overshadowed by that of Confucianism. In Japan it became wedded to Shinto beliefs about the great gods of nature and, as in China, it was also subject to the influence of Confucian ethics.

Mahayana is such a diverse movement, almost a family of religions in itself, that it is difficult to highlight its most widely-accepted characteristics. The place to begin is with the question of what happened to Buddha. In orthodox Theravada he was (and remains) a teacher, great above all others, but still essentially a man who taught and exemplified the truth. In Mahayana the human Buddha increasingly receded from sight. He was glorified, swallowed up in divinity, so that the Lotus Scripture, the most-loved of Mahayana writings, is presented as the message of Buddha seen as a transcendent being, eternal and sovereign over the world. This sort of Buddhism was patently religious; Buddha partook of divinity, and worship and prayer could be directed to him.

The contrast between Mahayana and Theravada is further seen in Mahayana's devotion to the Bodhisattva or being of wisdom. Mahayana taught that the saint could delay entry into nirvana for the sake of those still struggling on earth. Out of compassion a saint could become their spiritual benefactor, a supernatural spiritual being who could graciously respond to those who called upon him. Many passages in the Mahayana books speak about the vow of the Bodhisattva who resolves to be a saviour and to share the struggles of those enmeshed in ignorance.

> I take upon myself the burden of sorrow; I resolve to do so; I endure it all. I endure it all. I do not turn back or run away. I do not tremble...I am not afraid...nor do I despair. Assuredly, I must bear the burdens of all beings...for I have resolved to save them all. I must set them all free. I must save the whole world from the forest of birth, old age, disease, and rebirth, from misfortune and sin, from the round of birth and death, from the toils of heresy...For all beings are caught in the net of craving, encompassed by ignorance, held by the desire for existence; they are doomed to destruction, shut in a cage of pain...; they are ignorant, untrustworthy, full of doubts, always at loggerheads with one another, always prone to see evil; they cannot find a refuge in the ocean of existence; they are all on the edge of the gulf of destruction.
>
> Instructions of Akshayamati

The fertile soil of Mahayana produced a lush growth of Bodhisattvas. It was believed that many had attained Buddhahood (or enlightenment) not only in the present but also in the past ages. More Buddhas would come in future ages. In theory any person could become a Bodhisattva, take the vow and join the heavenly host. In fact, few Bodhisattvas are identifiable as successful saints. The connection with history became so slender that even the historicity of Buddha himself faded in importance. In China, and later in Japan, non-Buddhist deities were incorporated into Buddhist worship and regarded as Bodhisattvas. The ready application of this concept to indigenous divinities made Mahayana a most hospitable religion. The result was a Buddhism with an abundance of saviours. It became indeed the 'great vehicle', offering people a god or goddess for every season and every need.

Mahayana and the moral life

The transformation of Buddhism in North-East Asia into something very different from that accepted further south resulted in new ideas about how people should live and with what resources.

Mahayana changed the whole context of the moral life. It did this by saying that the struggle to change our existence did not depend on us alone. There were saviours whose help we could seek. The concept of divine grace became prominent in Mahayana. Salvation was seen less and less as a human achievement, a prize earned after a prolonged battle with craving. It became a boon bestowed on those who put their trust in a heavenly being. One way of showing the intensity of that trust was by the repetition of the saviour's name. Sects grew up in which the most pious act was the chanting of a formula such as 'Hail to the Name of Amida Buddha'. Those words are known in Japan as the *nembutsu,* and for seven hundred years at least they have been used to invoke the assistance of the saviour, Amida.

A change in the understanding of the religious goal, nirvana, went along with this belief in saving gods. For Theravada Buddhism, nirvana is not a place, not a heaven to which the soul goes on the death of the body. It is an experience that cannot be described. In Mahayana on the other hand, *Sukhavati,* 'the Pure Land' or 'the Happy Land', lay at the end of the human journey. For many sects expectations of a blessed life in a world beyond the grave became the central feature of their teaching. The promises of Amida were all-embracing; in this life the believer could call upon him for succour and in the next Amida would reward his worshippers with everlasting happiness.

> He never fails
> To reach the Lotus Land of Bliss
> Who calls,
> If only once,
> The name of Amida.
> A far, far distant land
> Is Paradise.
> I've heard them say
> But those who want to go
> Can reach there in a day.

The morality of Mahayana, however, was never permitted to be the only or dominant force shaping the behaviour of Buddhists. Confucianism affected the attitudes of all classes in China and, in certain periods, in Japan. Mahayana and Taoism satisfied religious needs; people found their ethical guidelines in Confucius. Some elements of original Buddhism were retained in Mahayana. In both China and Japan, the monastic order survived and the tradition of meditation persisted in the Chan sects of China and in Zen Buddhism in Japan.

Mahayana today

Japan is now a vital centre of Mahayana Buddhism. Ever since its introduction from Korea in the seventh century, Buddhism has intermingled with Shinto, absorbing the indigenous gods as Bodhisattvas. This is called Ryobu, 'two faced' Shinto; thus most Japanese have been Buddhists *and* Shintoists. On the whole Japanese Buddhism has been this-worldly, certainly more so than Theravada, and at times thoroughly nationalistic, endorsing the strongly patriotic attitudes fostered by the mythology and worship of Shinto.

The most significant of the Mahayana sects, which has flourished in Japan since 1945, is *Soka Gakkai*. It claims a growth from 20 000 families in 1952 to about 6 million today. Its main text is the Lotus Scripture and it regards a thirteenth century preacher, Nichiren, as the true Buddha for the present age. Despite its dogmatic claim for the finality of Nichiren's exposition of Buddhism, Soka Gakkai has much of the traditional pliancy of Mahayana. It incorporates elements drawn from Shintoism and Christianity. Its deviation from the stern non-materialistic morality of Theravada is seen most clearly in what it promises those who join its movement and perform the duties of membership. Buddhahood is often described as the goal of every believer. Buddhahood is happiness, but the important thing for *Soka Gakkai* is that, as long as people are in this world, wealth and prosperity, success in business, escape from accidents (to cite a few examples from testimonials) will be theirs. This Mahayana sect does not concern itself with craving, with making people aware of the delusory character of the world's gifts. Rather it encourages people to believe, to chant the opening lines of the Lotus Scripture so that more of this world's benefits may be theirs. Buddhism in this movement has capitulated to the pressures of Asia's most prosperous society.

Buddhist attitudes to the environment

Buddhism is unlike the Jewish-Christian tradition with its doctrine that the world was created by God and the responsibility for it given to humankind. Buddha refused to speculate on creation; rather he taught that all things are characterised by *anicca* or impermanence. The human quest in Theravada is liberation from worldly materialism, from treating the world as real and substantial. Against such a background it is not surprising that environmental issues do not at present loom large in Buddhist communities. They are irrelevant to the primary concern of Buddha's thinking which was to break our bondage to the world and the craving that it engenders. This negation of the world at the core of the Buddhist religious tradition provides little restraint on the modernising forces in Buddhist societies such as Thailand which are intent on the economic development of natural resources. It may well be that concern about ecology arises in such societies because of the human effects of exploitation, but it is unlikely that the inspiration for this will come from the dominant religion.

Some current issues

As far as medical ethics are concerned the two most important Buddhist ideas are its view of human life and its ethical teaching on non-violence towards all creatures. According to Theravada Buddhism a human being consists of five elements or *skandas* of which the body is the most obvious. These are in a state of constant change. Beyond them there is no enduring soul or ego that survives death. Such an idea is a form of illusion. What happens when a person dies is that the elements disintegrate and another combination comes into existence, the nature of which is determined by the merit built up by *karma* in the previous life. There is, in this sense, rebirth but it is not a soul that is reborn.

Despite this idea of the essential transience of all beings, life is to be treated kindly. There are references in early Buddhist literature to the setting up of hospitals for the treatment of both humans and animals. Disease was seen as an impediment to the quest for enlightenment although detachment from the world, cultivated by meditation, meant that eventual death was accepted with serenity. One of the steps on the Eightfold Path was Right Conduct. This included the obligation to refrain from doing harm to living beings. The strict Buddhist is unlikely to approve of either abortion or contraception. Most major ethical issues in medicine today arise because of society's possession of advanced medical technology. Such is not yet the case in Theravada countries. In Burma, for example, the widespread provision of basic services is still the goal, especially in rural areas. Advanced technology is, of course, present in Japan but the degree to which Buddhist ethics influence that society is slight compared with Theravada countries. Birth control and abortion are widely accepted. Secular considerations are likely to be most influential in debates in Japan regarding the application of medical technology.

Women in Buddhism

With regard to the status of women in Buddhism it appears that originally Buddha gave the same teachings to both males and females, presented the same goal of enlightenment to both and established separate monastic orders (the *sangha*) for both monks and nuns. In Buddhist history, however, the accent has been on the male order. The number of nuns or female ascetics has been very small compared with the vastly larger membership of the male *sangha*. It is the latter that has been regarded as superior and entrusted with the responsibility for teaching the doctrine. Monks could teach nuns but not the other way around. It was argued by some that the inferior status of females was due to bad *karma* from a previous existence. The situation in Theravada countries has been that the leadership of Buddhism, under the patronage of a pious king, was in the hands of the monks within their *sangha*. The few women who have engaged in the advanced religious quest have been seen as a minor appendage to the male order.

Outside the *sangha* the religious functions of women in

154

Buddhist households have been to tend the shrines, to encourage respect for the doctrine and, above all, to earn merit, especially by the provision of food each morning to the monks. Modern education will in time change the social status of women in Buddhist countries but the values bequeathed by the past are deeply entrenched and rapid change is unlikely.

We append a final note on the present-day growth of interest in Buddhism outside its Asian homelands. In recent years Buddhism has won a number of converts in Western countries. The reasons for its appeal are many and complex—its humanism, its claim to encourage world peace (although Buddhist countries have armies and go to war against each other), its promise of inward tranquillity, and the challenge it presents to the hedonistic and materialistic societies of the West. Buddhism is a thorough-going alternative to the religious views of life that have shaped Western thinking through the centuries. It is also an alternative to the dominant value-systems of Western culture.

6
Confucianism

This is the ancient Chinese
symbol of the two cosmic
forces, yang and yin. These two
powers, male and female, are
complementary. All things
reflect their interaction. Human
life should also display a
harmony akin to that of yang
and yin.

Main dates of Chinese religion

		BCE
Early beliefs and rituals	▼	1500
Beginnings of later Five Classics	▼	1000
		600
Lao-tzu (?)		
Confucius		551
Tao Te Ching		
Spread of Confucian thought		400
Debates with rival views		
Mencius, the champion of Confucian orthodoxy		300
Confucianism endorsed by the		
emperor and made basis of education		100
		CE
Entry of Buddhism		200
Taoism expands, Lao-tzu deified		600
State cult of Confucius;	▼	
sacrifices offered to him		
Neo-Confucian philosophers;		
opposition to Buddhism and Taoism	▼	1000
Confucianism, the dominant		
philosophy of the governing elite	▼	1500
Impact of West begins		1800
Abolition of Confucian		
examination system for officials		1906
Revolution, end of Confucian State		1911
Triumph of Communism		1949

Never do to others what you would not like them to do to you.

Confucianism

The teachings about humankind and society associated with the Chinese sage, Confucius, were a dominant influence on the culture of East Asia until recent times. Not only in China was Confucius regarded as the fount of all truth in matters of human behaviour; in Vietnam, Korea and Japan he was also revered as the wisest of all human teachers. But in China today Confucius and his moral teaching are spurned. A new ideology derived from Marxism is being extolled as the light of the world. It is probably too early to say what will happen to Confucianism, one of the main ingredients of Chinese culture for two thousand years. It may prove ineradicable because it was for so long the most important thread woven into the fabric of Chinese identity. On the other hand, Chinese communists have determined since 1949 to make a break with the past. The Chinese future must, in their view, be very different from the Chinese past. In pursuit of this goal, the Communist rulers of the country have explicitly rejected the moral and social legacy of Confucianism. The great teacher of the sixth century BCE, honoured above all others for more than a score of generations, is now regarded by many as a contaminating and corrupting influence. Confucius, it is said, was a supporter of a feudalistic and hierarchical society, an advocate of government by an élite, an opponent of social change. What can such a person contribute to a China determined to make all things new? The answer, according to many in modern China, is: nothing.

The moral philosophy of Confucius may be destined to disappear or to survive with much less power than it had in past centuries. Even if this is so, it is still worth looking at what Confucius had to say. Confucianism is certainly of historical interest in that it was a formative force in East Asian civilisation for over two thousand years. To understand it is to understand much about China and to understand the peculiar character of the confrontation that has taken place in the last century and a half between China and the ideologies of the West. Confucianism is one of many answers to the question of what ideals we should seek and what sort of society we should build. Some people, without being Confucians, affirm that there are insights and values in the Chinese tradition that could be incorporated into other cultures.

Confucianism and religion

Writers on Confucius sometimes present him as an ethical teacher with little or no interest in religion. According to this view, he was not concerned with a transcendent morality or the will of a god or gods, but rather with elucidating the principles on which a harmonious and stable society could be based. He was a social reformer. He described what a community could become and gave advice and encouragement to those who wanted to see their world changed.

Confucius was undoubtedly this-worldly. It was *this* world, *this* human society, people as they are in *this* life that occupied his attention. At the same time he taught that the way people should walk was the Way of Heaven itself. Heaven both willed and made possible the pursuit of goodness. Society depended for its health on the continuous realisation by its members of a lofty ethical idealism. But virtue was not only what a society needed; it was also what the Supreme Being, Heaven, had ordained that people should seek. Later we will return to the question of Confucius' religion and the extent to which it supported his ethical system.

Some centuries after the death of Confucius, a set of beliefs and rituals, a religion, developed to which the term 'Confucianism' is attached. Much of it pre-dated Confucius—the offering of sacrifices and prayers to the gods of nature, the honouring of the two great deities of Heaven and Earth, the performance of rituals associated with the ancestral spirits of clans and families. In time temples were built in honour of Confucius himself, and a religious cult developed in which he was the object of prayer and sacrifice. From about the third century CE Chinese religion was an amalgam of the very ancient beliefs of the people, the gods of Taoism, the saints and saviours of Mahayana Buddhism, and Confucianism. The distinctive contribution of Confucius to this phenomenon lay in the ethical teachings associated with his name.

It is possible in theory to separate the strands in the pattern of Chinese belief and behaviour, but it is doubtful whether this was often done in practice. A person in need went to the shrine of any god—Taoist or Buddhist—that might be able to offer help. Religion was a syncretism, a mixture in which the primary ethical element came from Confucianism. There was, however, a relatively small group of Chinese who looked with disdain at popular religion. For them what mattered most in life was the cultivation of the Confucian virtues. These Confucians comprised the ruling class and the landed gentry of China. They might offer sacrifice on the altars of the ancestors and share, as officials, in the rituals carried out in temples. But they kept their distance from what they considered the crudities of popular religion. The Confucianism of the scholar-gentry class was agnostic about religious questions such as the nature of the divine and the fate of the individual after death. It was not without its rituals and ceremonies, as the innumerable Confucian temples attest, but its concerns were ethical rather than doctrinal, practical rather than mystical, and focussed on behaviour rather than on belief.

Confucius: heritage and legacy

'Confucius' is the Latinised form of the Chinese title, Kung Fu-tzu, 'Master Kung', by which the teacher has been known for many centuries. Little can be said for certain about his life and teachings. The Analects or selected sayings of Confucius, one of the primary sources, is usually dated seventy or eighty years after his death. In this, as in other germinal Confucian works, it is not always possible to distinguish between the Confucius of history and a Confucius explained and embellished by his faithful followers.

The usual account of his life places his birth at 551 BCE in the small Chinese province of Shantung. China was then divided into a number of states, often at war with each other; many were also subject to internal conflict due to rival aspirants for position and power. Confucius saw this chaos as just the opposite of what China should be and of what China had been in past ages. He became convinced that he had a message which, if it were heeded by rulers and others in authority, could banish the strife that was disfiguring the face of society. It is possible that in early manhood Confucius held minor offices within the state of Lu. Later, according to tradition, he became a magistrate. But Lu was a very small state and Confucius seems to have sought a much wider influence. He spent some years as an itinerant teacher, visiting rulers and gathering around him a group of disciples. Towards the end of his life he returned to Lu, where he died in 479 BCE.

The traditions about Confucius present him as a person with a lifelong interest in education, especially education for leadership. This was not synonymous with book knowledge. The intellect was subordinated to the practical—a person of learning knew how to live. Confucius studied the Five Classics, an assortment of stories from ancient Chinese history, poetry, ritual and court records. In their final form the books are later than Confucius but the originals probably existed in his lifetime. Such study had a moral value in that open-hearted students could be influenced by edifying accounts of the lives of former leaders. Confucius was thus very conscious of his heritage. The past could guide the present. He was a revivalist rather than an innovator, a restorer of tried and tested values rather than the founder of a new ethical philosophy.

An important aspect of his teaching was his appeal to the example of a number of sage-kings who had ruled China in previous dynasties. He believed that under their benevolent rule all classes lived in harmony. People did their duty towards their neighbours and received in turn the service which was due to them. These wise rulers may, in fact, be legendary, but their example had a great influence on the teaching of Confucius. Their example was also partly responsible for his optimistic view of human society. The golden age of the past would return in China if only people would walk the way of the ancients. What was achieved once could be realised again. People had the capacity and, with the right sort of education, they could be given the will to transform their world.

The heritage of Confucius included religion and its visible expression in rites and ceremonies. It seems clear from the Analects and other early Confucian accounts that Confucius was not a questioner in matters of religion. He did not probe such matters as the nature of God, Heaven, the power of the spirits or the state of the dead. But he did speak of the Way of Heaven and he saw his own heart's harmony with Heaven as the climax of his life.

> The Master said: At fifteen I set my heart upon learning. At thirty, I had planted my feet firm upon the ground. At forty, I no longer suffered from perplexities. At fifty, I knew what were the biddings of Heaven. At sixty, I heard them with docile ear. At seventy, I could follow the dictates of my own heart; for what I desired no longer overstepped the boundaries of right.
>
> Analects 2: 4*

Ritual became enormously important in later Confucianism. In his own time there were already long-established ceremonies centering around the ancestors and unseen spiritual beings. The Book of Rites, one of the five classics, contains material from before his time. In one passage in the Analects it is suggested that the wise man worship and offer sacrifices that will keep the spirits at a distance to prevent them from harming people.

> Fan Ch'ih asked about wisdom. The Master said, He who devotes himself to securing for his subjects what it is right they should have, who by respect for the Spirits keeps them at a distance, may be termed wise.
>
> Analects 6: 20

On ritual veneration of ancestors, a verse in the Analects says:

> The Master said, High office filled by men of narrow views, ritual performed without reverence, the forms of mourning observed without grief—these are things I cannot bear to see.
>
> Analects 3: 26

Another passage indicates, however, that the living have priority over the dead:

> Tzu-lu asked how one should serve ghosts and spirits. The Master said, Till you have learnt to serve men, how can you serve ghosts? Tzu-lu then ventured upon a question about the dead. The Master said, Till you know about the living, how are you to know about the dead?
>
> Analects 11: 11

*Quotations in this chapter are taken from A. Waley (tr.) *The Analects of Confucius*, George Allen & Urwin, London, 1949.

From the sayings attributed to Confucius it is clear that he was not regarded as an iconoclast. He did not repudiate rituals hallowed by generations of piety, but believed their observance was necessary and valued the sincerity of those who shared in them. Yet the main concern of Confucius' ethical system was clearly the state of the world. Ritual in any religion can become an end in itself or a substitute for serious ethical concern. With his deep respect for the past Confucius accepted the beliefs and practices that had come down from former times. But he was sure that the pursuit of goodness took precedence over everything else.

For some time after the death of Confucius in 479 BCE his teaching was under attack from rivals who were hostile to his view of humankind and to the ethical principles that he expounded. His legacy was by no means assured. It was preserved by his disciples, notably Mencius, who both defended and developed what had come from Confucius. The socio-ethical tradition, Confucianism, finally won the endorsement of an emperor of the Han dynasty in the second century BCE. In later centuries the imperial favour was sometimes withdrawn and given to Taoism or Buddhism but Confucianism survived such periods of eclipse and was restored as the ideology underpinning the Chinese state. It filled this role up to the early years of this century until, with the republican revolution of 1911, it was swept aside as an inadequate foundation for a modern country.

The virtue of goodness

Confucianism was a living movement for two thousand years and in the course of this long history it developed many features. Some of these are more clearly present than others in the early literature. Some are the amplification and elaboration of ideas expressed in incipient form by Confucius. It is impossible to draw a clear line between

Confucius and the tradition that bears his name. In much of the teaching we cannot be certain how much comes from the sage and how much was due to the disciples' reflection on his words.

We begin our summary of the Confucian ethical system by looking at the virtue of *jen* (or *ren*) 'goodness'. Goodness, in later Chinese tradition, was regarded as the root of four other virtues—justice, religious and moral propriety, wisdom and faithfulness. It was also taught that goodness was an expression of our true nature. It distinguished the life of human beings from that of the animals. To achieve goodness was to be truly natural, to manifest the essential meaning of being human. Furthermore, Confucians said that goodness was a goal that could be realised. People did not have to struggle against an inherited bias towards evil. Nor did they have to call upon the grace of a supernatural being in order to become what they could be. Self-discipline, the study of the lives of worthy ancestors, persistent moral steadfastness—by such self-saving methods they could rise above the debasing power of selfish desire and so demonstrate the quality of *jen*, an inward integrity as well as an outward righteousness.

Goodness is a blank-cheque word; it has to be filled in and given a content. *Jen* is sometimes translated by terms such as benevolence, compassion and human-heartedness. In the Analects Confucius does not analyse the concept of goodness. He shows that a 'good man' (he applies the term only to males), a man who pursues *jen*, has certain characteristics. He dislikes no one, considers the feelings of others, and is courteous to all. He honours his ancestors and is loyal in all his relationships. He is so intent on following what is right that he is not distracted by material comfort or material distress.

> The Master said, Without Goodness a man
> Cannot for long endure adversity,
> Cannot for long enjoy prosperity.

The Good Man rests content with Goodness; he that is merely wise pursues Goodness in the belief that it pays to do so.

Wealth and rank are what every man desires; but if they can only be retained to the detriment of the Way he professes, he must relinquish them. Poverty and obscurity are what every man detests, but if they can only be avoided to the detriment of the Way he professes, he must accept them. The gentleman who ever parts company with Goodness does not fulfil that name. Never for a moment does a gentleman quit the way of Goodness. He is never so harried but that he cleaves to this: never so tottering but that he cleaves to this.

Analects 4: 2, 5

Fan Ch'ih asked about Goodness. The Master said, In private life, courteous, in public life, diligent, in relationships, loyal. This is a maxim that no matter where you may be, even amid the barbarians of the east or north, may never be set aside.

Analects 13: 19

Later Confucianism, as we have said, held a very optimistic view of human nature: goodness is within reach. In the Analects, however, Confucius himself is far from hopeful about the possibility of becoming a man of goodness. He speaks of goodness as a characteristic of the great sage-kings of the past; it is a very lofty ideal. Yet even in Confucius, goodness is not so transcendent that it is pointless for people to seek it. The Confucian *chun-tzu*, or 'gentleman' sets his heart upon goodness and partially, at least, he evidences it in his relationships with other people.

The practice of reciprocity

One obvious expression of goodness is the practice of *shu*, 'reciprocity or mutual consideration'. This is the golden rule for interpersonal relationships and it has a special relevance for rulers who have to deal with the affairs of their subjects.

Tzu-kung asked, saying, Is there any single saying that one can act upon all day and every day? The Master said, Perhaps the saying about consideration. Never do to others what you would not like them to do to you.

Analects 15: 23

Jan Jung asked about Goodness. The Master said, Behave when away from home as though you were in the presence of an important guest. Deal with the common people as though you were officiating at an important sacrifice. Do not do to others what you would not like yourself. Then there will be no feelings of opposition to you, whether it is the affairs of a State that you are handling or the affairs of a family.

Analects 12: 2

The good man, in the teaching of the Analects, is enmeshed with his fellows in a network of duties and privileges. He can expect to receive from others; but he must also give. Mutual consideration should permeate all human relationships. This is the right way because it is the surest means of dispelling tension and fostering good will.

The Confucian emphasis on mutual consideration, on a 'give-and-receive' morality, was amplified in the description of Five Relationships. They constitute the essential structure of a person's life as a member of communities. It is doubtful whether the full-scale scheme of Five Relationships (and the attitudes which they involve) comes from Confucius himself. The scheme appears in the Book of Rites which, although it may contain early material, is dated two or three centuries after Confucius. It must be read in the context of a patriarchal society.

The Five Relationships and the attitudes they involve can be set out as follows:

Father	Is kind Gives protection Provides education	Shows respect Accepts father's guidance Cares for him in old age and performs the custom- ary burial ceremonies	Son
Elder brother	Sets an example of refinement and good behaviour	Respects the character and experience of the elder	Younger brother
Husband	Carries out his family duties Is honourable and faithful Provides for his wife and family	Looks after the home Is obedient Diligently meets the needs of her husband and children	Wife
Elder	Gives encouragement Shows consideration towards younger people Sets a good example	Shows respect Defers to the advice of those with more experience Is eager to learn	Junior
Ruler	Acts justly Strives to improve the welfare of his people Is worthy of loyalty	Are loyal Serve their ruler Honour their ruler because of his position and character	Subjects

Three of these relationships belong to the family. Confucian teaching has, without question, had an enormous influence on Chinese family life. Both parents and children, young and old, had responsibilities to each other. The faithful fulfilment of these gave security, stability and continuity to the family. Beyond the family was the clan and beyond that the nation. Confucianism encouraged loyalty to the nation and sometimes likened it to a family of which the emperor was the father. But the main stress was on the virtues and attitudes that would enhance daily life. A man's loyalty to his family was seen in all his actions, his sacrifices at the ancestral shrine, his readiness to marry someone deemed suitable by his elders. A man accepted the wisdom taught by his father and in turn passed it on to his son.

A sense of order pervaded the Confucian family. Each member knew his or her place in relation to others and knew what that place involved. To belong to such a family might seem to us a very restrictive and stultifying experience. Whether it was felt to be so would depend on a person's expectations. It is not surprising that the Communist Party in China sometimes seeks to undermine this traditional view of the family. A good Communist deprecates intense loyalty to the family and the clan. What matters in the new China of today is that a person should serve the state, the people.

The cultivation of filial piety

The pre-eminence of the family and the cult of ancestors in Chinese society existed before Confucius. It is likely that those who first heard the sayings from the Analects about honouring parents did not regard them as very novel; rather, they were a reiteration of what had long been accepted as fit and proper attitudes.

In the generations after Confucius, however, respect for parents or filial piety, to use the common phrase, was so raised in status that for some teachers it was the most desirable of all moral qualities. Such 'piety' consisted of love and respect for parents, the acceptance of their wishes and concern for their welfare, solicitude for the family fortunes and, hopefully, the birth of children (especially sons) who would ensure the family's continuance. The Classic of Filial Piety was compiled some three centuries after Confucius and contains explicit teaching about this virtue. In the Analects itself several passages show that Confucius endorsed the long-standing practice of honouring parents, both in life and in death.

Meng I Tzu asked about the treatment of parents. The Master said, Never disobey. When Fan Ch'ih was driving his carriage for him, the Master said, Meng asked me about the treatment of parents and I said, Never disobey. Fan Ch'ih said, In what sense did you mean it? The Master said, While they are alive, serve them according to ritual and sacrifice to them according to ritual.

Meng Wu Po asked about the treatment of parents. The Master said, Behave in such a way that your father and mother have no anxiety about you, except concerning your health.

Tzu-yu asked about the treatment of parents. The Master said, 'Filial sons' nowadays are people who see to it that their parents get enough to eat. But even dogs and horses are cared for to that extent. If there is no feeling of respect, wherein lies the difference?

Analects 2: 5–7

The Master said, In serving his father and mother a man may gently remonstrate with them. But if he sees that he has failed to change their opinion, he should resume an attitude of deference and not thwart them, he may feel discouraged, but not resentful.

Analects 4: 18

Expositions of filial piety usually stressed the home as the natural soil for the generation and growth of moral qualities. People could not grow in *jen* or goodness if they were not respectful towards their parents or if they did not show concern towards other members of the family. No conflict was seen between this focus on parents and cultivation of civic virtues. Filial piety was natural to human beings. Children showed a spontaneous love towards their parents. Moral education built upon this disposition so that respect for parents grew into respect for authorities beyond the family.

Men of merit

One of the most important as well as most enduring figures in Chinese history is the *chun-tzu* or Confucian 'gentleman'. He appears in the literature of Confucius as a member of the ruling class who seriously pursues wisdom and cultivates personal goodness. He may be conscious that he stands apart from the common people but pride and arrogance have no part in his behaviour. His manner is calm, considered and characterised by an avoidance of extremes. He follows the principle of the mean, a middle way between, for example, an inordinate love of luxury and an ascetic disdain for this world's pleasures. As a gentleman, he honours those who have gone before him and transmits a worthwhile legacy to those who come after him. He neither flatters rulers nor fears them; he always strives to do what is right, to uphold the Way of Heaven.

The gentleman is thoroughly conscientious.

> Master K'ung said, The gentleman has nine cares. In seeing he is careful to see clearly, in hearing he is careful to hear distinctly, in his looks he is careful to be kindly; in his manner to be respectful, in his words to be loyal, in his work to be diligent. When in doubt he is careful to ask for information; when angry he has a care for the consequences, and when he sees a chance of gain, he thinks carefully whether the pursuit of it would be consonant with the Right.
>
> Analects 16: 10

He is concerned about the people for whom he is responsible.

> Tzu-lu asked about the qualities of a true gentleman. The Master said, He cultivates in himself the capacity to be diligent in his tasks. Tzu-lu said, Can he not go further than that? The Master said, He cultivates in himself the capacity to ease the lot of other people. Tzu-lu said, Can he not go further than that? The Master said, He cultivates in himself the capacity to ease the lot of the whole populace.
>
> Analects 14: 45

> The Master said, A gentleman in his dealings with the world has neither enmities nor affections; but wherever he sees Right he ranges himself beside it.
>
> The Master said, A gentleman takes as much trouble to discover what is right as lesser men take to discover what will pay.
>
> Analects 4: 10–16

> There are three things that a gentleman, in following the Way,
> places above all the rest; from every attitude, every gesture that he
> employs he must remove all trace of violence or arrogance; every
> look that he composes in his face must betoken good faith; from
> every word that he utters, from every intonation, he must remove
> all trace of coarseness or impropriety.

Analects 8: 4

The 'gentleman' in China was of historical importance because officials were selected on the basis of their study of the Confucian writings and their exemplification of the Confucian virtues. For centuries, right down to 1906, administrators were chosen through a series of examinations in the classics. Such 'men of merit' had to be morally, as well as intellectually, fit for the work of administration. This class of scholar-administrators naturally looked to the past and to the distant past at that. This conservatism, combined with the belief that China was culturally superior to all other nations, made it difficult for them to come to terms with the vastly different civilisation of the West. When the dynamic, exploitative countries of the West came to the Far East in the early years of the nineteenth century, Chinese officialdom, steeped in Confucianism, was at a grave disadvantage. It was unable to appropriate values and ideas from the West. Every Chinese defeat from 1840 onwards eroded the authority of the traditional ruling class and the ideology it embodied. In the eyes of nationalists (and later Communists) Confucianism had to be ignored or rejected and people with modern ideas had to replace the Confucian gentlemen as the leaders of China's future.

Three further things should be said about the Confucian 'men of merit'. Confucius taught that privilege does entail responsibilities. He saw society divided into classes, notably the common people and the nobility. And he held that authority had to be exercised by a few over the many. There are enough passages, however, to show that Confucius was aware of the arrogance and avarice to which people of privilege are prone. The good man, the gentleman, knows that nothing must deflect him from seeking what is right. This means that he will not exploit his position, nor the respect that it evinces among the less privileged. His moral sense will bind together in his soul a humble acceptance of privilege and awareness of his own stewardship.

The second implication of the concept of 'men of merit' is that the character of society as a whole will depend on the moral witness of its leadership.

> The essence of the gentleman is that of wind; the essence of small people is that of grass.
> And when a wind passes over the grass it cannot choose but bend.
> If you desire what is good the people will at once be good.
>
> Analects 11: 19

Example was considered the most important means of maintaining the moral health of society, and the example of rulers and officials was especially important. Let people be moral, let individuals seek goodness and, like centres of light, they will eventually illumine the whole of their world. Social activism in the modern sense of an organised campaign to rid society of evil is not part of the Confucian tradition.

The purpose of education was to produce 'gentlemen'. Education in China always had, as one of its primary aims, the development of character. For Confucius education meant the study of the past, the performance of ritual, training in music, and grounding in the moral principles that held people together in a community. The goal was to produce a class of people of incorruptible character who were fit to rule others.

Each in his place

There are two terms used in Confucianism which sum up most of what has been said.

The first is 'the rectification of names', 'name' meaning the position a person occupies or the role a person must perform. Trouble erupts in a community when people forget their 'names', and fail to fulfil their appointed roles. There was discord in China in Confucius' day because this had happened. A 'rectification of names' implies restoration of the correct understanding of relationships, of what it means, for example, to be a ruler or a subject. The ideal social order comes about when people, in each of their relationships, do what is appropriate and fitting.

The second term is *li*. This is translated in a variety of ways—ritual, propriety, decorum, good manners, and proper conduct. Originally it denoted the ritual associated with gods and the spirits of ancestors. Rituals were fixed: there was a proper ritual for a particular religious purpose and there was a correct way of carrying out that ritual. Some rituals were appropriate for a specific occasion; some were not. Education should give people the capacity to discriminate between them.

From its origins in the ceremonial life of ancient China, *li* came to denote appropriate behaviour in the basic relationships of life. It included what we call etiquette but went further than this to cover both behaviour and attitudes. A truly educated person acted spontaneously according to *li*. Such a person displayed the demeanour, looked, spoke, and replied in a way appropriate for the occasion. The 'gentleman' knew that there was always a fit and proper way of dealing with people.

Some Confucians identified *li* with the *tao* or 'Way' ordained by Heaven. They believed that harmony, the inevitable result of everybody acting with propriety, was a cosmic law. It was *meant* to be the pattern of life. This accent on harmony also accorded with the very old Chinese belief in two primary forces within the universe, yang and yin. All that is has come into being through the interaction of these two complementary powers; the one male and dynamic; the other, female and passive. All is well in nature and in the life of humankind if the two operate harmoniously. Nature becomes destructive and human life disordered if this harmony is absent. Harmony—in the soul of the individual and in dealings with others—is what the universe wills. This is also the message of Confucius.

A horizontal ethic

Most ethical teaching is concerned with human relations, with the way people should treat their neighbours and how society should be ordered. Some ethical systems are strongly transcendental or vertical—it is God's law that should determine what people do; it is in obedience to God's will that they find fulfilment. Despite its acknowledgement of an ultimate cosmic law, it is clear that the ethics of Confucius are more horizontal than vertical. Although he believed that what was right was grounded in the nature of things, in the tao or Way of Heaven, his primary interest was in the social benefits that would flow from the application of his principles.

Confucius does not appeal to other-worldly sanctions. He offers no promise of a blessed afterlife to those who act rightly and no threat of hell to those who are perverse and disobedient. There are no law-giving gods or goddesses sending their commandments down to people and addressing them with the directness of a ruler confronting a servant. Life for Confucius is to be lived with a high sense of seriousness, not because of a future judgement before a divine being but because people are beings of such dignity and stature that they ought to realise the moral potentialities inherent in their nature. By doing so they will enrich themselves and their society.

Confucius' ethic is also horizontal in its lack of a profound doctrine of human sinfulness. He was well aware that people could turn away from goodness. (Was not this the trouble in China in his own day?) But he was sure that his advice *could* be taken, that people *could* be educated to seek virtue, that they *could* transform their world. Because there is no strong sense of a personal god in Confucianism, and because people are seen as failing rather than sinning, there is no teaching about human penitence and divine forgiveness.

Also absent is the conception of divine resources, of an empowering grace, upon which people can draw to become what they hope to be.

What the fate of this Chinese ethical tradition will be is an intriguing question. Modern China rejects it as upholding class attitudes that must be extirpated. It can be argued, however, that elements of Confucianism have in fact been carried over into the new ideology; for example, the belief in the capacity to transform society and the overriding importance of social harmony.

Environmental issues in China

In the last forty years Chinese society has been so moulded by Marxist ideology that it is virtually impossible to establish a significant continuing influence from the country's ancestral religious traditions. This is especially the case when one remembers that at certain times since the Communist triumph in 1949 the government has supported campaigns against the teaching and practice of religion. It is unlikely that China's three religions—Taoism, Buddhism and Confucianism—are now sufficiently vigorous to contribute values and ideas to any debate, for example, that may arise regarding ecology and environmental issues. Economic development and the drive to establish a modern society in China will raise such issues but, given the prevailing non-religious ideology of the regime, they will be debated on pragmatic and humanistic grounds.

Some current issues

China has a long history of indigenous medicine of which acupuncture is the feature best known in the West. As in most peasant societies, people believed that disease was caused by demonic forces; cures therefore involved propitiating supernatural powers and treatment by herbal remedies. As well as this, the Chinese developed a sophisticated and, to most Westerners, mysterious understanding of energy flows or *chi* within the body which they manipulated by a variety of means, including acupuncture.

Taoism stressed the importance of living in harmony with the tao or Way of nature so that health was seen as not only a matter of the body but also of the soul or mind. In recent decades Western scientific medicine has become more important, allied with contributions from the indigenous tradition. As in all developing countries there tends to be a gulf between what services are available in big cities and in the rural areas. In recent years the government has sponsored programmes to deal with basic health in areas of greatest need. Bioethical issues will be debated in China, like those of the environment, on secular and social grounds. The contribution of the surviving religions is not likely to be significant.

Women in China

One of the most striking social changes effected under Communism has been in the status of women. In Confucian society women were identified with the yin or passive principle in the cosmos. They had their roles, not least as mothers contributing through birth to the ongoing life of the family and clan, but they were subservient to males who embodied the yang or active principle. They were seen as essentially upholders of the family while only the Confucian trained 'gentlemen' could aspire to leadership in the wider society. The male members of the household presided over clan ceremonies at, for example, the funerals of members and at those honouring the ancestors. Confucian society was patriarchal and the lesser status of women was symbolised by such practices as foot-binding, female infanticide and the presence in rich households of concubines. Many reformers rejected Confucianism, seeing it not only as responsible for the status of women but as inimical to social change in general. The Communists saw the revolutionary potential of women and, on coming to power, instituted great changes in their status. As a result they have participated widely in the work force, and attained political office at the local as well as at higher levels. Divorce and abortion have been made easier.

What will happen to Confucian values and ideas in a developing China only the future can reveal. However discounted and opposed it may be at present, the legacy from China's greatest teacher will probably never be totally obliterated.

7
Australian Aboriginal religions

No single symbol is common to
the Aboriginal religions. These
concentric circles are typical.
They can depict the Aboriginal
view of the universe.

Some dates of Aboriginal history

	BCE
Aboriginal ancestors arrive in Australia	40 000
Archaeological evidence of ritual burial practices at Lake Mungo	▼ 26 000

	CE
White settlers arrive	1788
Aborigines placed in reserves	1900
Powerful influence of Christianity	
Aborigines given right to vote	1967
Aboriginal Land Rights Act (Northern Territory)	1976

Australian Aboriginal religions

The Australian Aborigines are a very religious people. For them, every feature of their land is sacred, all flora and fauna are sacred, all relationships have a sacred character. Between their everyday culture and their religious culture there is no distinction or the very vaguest line. Aboriginal languages do not even have a separate word for 'religion' so alien is the idea to them. Their religion has no founder; there are no sacred books. Aboriginal religion is very different from any other religious system you will find in this book. Today there are about fifty Aboriginal groups who have retained some continuity with the land from which they came. Some Aborigines have been converted, often forcibly, to Christianity; some have formed a hybrid between Christianity and their Aboriginal religion. Many urban Aborigines have lost their roots, both cultural and religious. We will be dealing with the Aboriginal groups in the past and the present who have retained their religious heritage. Over two hundred years ago the first white settlers found at least 600 groups and perhaps 300 000 Aborigines in the Australian continent. Where did they come from?

Recent archaeology has excavated camp sites, burial sites, sacred sites and art sites belonging to the Aborigines of the past. It has shown that the Aborigines have lived in Australia much longer than was ever envisaged before. At Lake Mungo in New South Wales the remains of a young female Aborigine were found and these have been dated back 26 000 years. She had been cremated and her bones crushed and placed in a conical hole. A male body was also found at Lake Mungo and dated back 30 000 years. The body had been embalmed with red ochre after death. Perhaps this was part of some religious ritual. In Western Australia at the Upper Swan centre there are tools and charcoal dating back 38 000 years. With such established centres as these dated to 38 000 years the Aborigines must have arrived in Australia at the very least 40 000 years ago, perhaps much earlier.

This would place their arrival at the end of the last Ice Age when about one-quarter of the earth's surface was covered with ice as against one-tenth at the moment. Since no pre-human remains have been found in Australia it is presumed that the Aborigines came by migration. Due to the ice cover, migration from Asia would have been easier but it would still have involved some significant boat journeys. Asia and Australia were never closer than 50–100 kilometres apart during the Ice Age. Perhaps the first landings were by chance when people were blown off course. Perhaps there were intentional migrations. Some scholars have conjectured that the migration would have been from Java to Timor to New Guinea (then still connected by land to Australia) or the Kimberley region.

Whichever way they arrived, the Aborigines managed to establish a way of life in harmony with an environment that Europeans regard as harsh. This involved their everyday life and their religion. When Captain Cook reported on them in 1770 he wrote, 'In reality, they are far happier than we Europeans...they live in tranquillity...they covet not...in my opinion they think themselves provided with all the necessaries of life.'

We will first look at a 'typical' Aboriginal religious system, remembering that there is no one single Aboriginal religion. Different groups have different religious systems, although there are some similarities. We will then attempt to describe an Aboriginal religious ethical system.

The Dreaming

At the very centre of Aboriginal religion is the key belief of the Dreaming. Aborigines from different groups will use different words for the Dreaming but it is a common concept throughout Aboriginal Australia. The Dreaming did not take place in time. It took place before there was time. The Dreaming describes, first of all, the great events of creation. Aborigines believe that before creation there was a formless substance. Sometimes this is depicted as a watery mass, at other times as a featureless and waterless desert. Spirit Beings or Ancestor Beings detached themselves from this formless substance and emerged in various forms. Sometimes the forms they assumed were human-like, at other times they were animal-like or bird-like or plant-like. Kangaroo-Man, Snake-Man, Bowerbird-Woman, Moon-Man were such Ancestor Beings.

Having distinguished themselves from the formless substance they travelled over the terrain, doing the sorts of things Aborigines would do or the sorts of things animals would do. As they travelled and performed various actions they transformed the entire landscape. From the formless substance there emerged trails, mountains, rocks, waterholes and other features, all shaped by the activity of the Ancestor Beings. Sometimes an Ancestor Being would leave behind the impression of his or her spiritual body in the shape of, for example, a river bed or a rocky ridge. Sometimes they would use weapons or tools and these would leave a geological feature. At other times the Ancestor Being was changed into a feature such as a significant rock outcrop. Other Ancestor Beings ascended into the skies when their travels were over. There they were transformed into the celestial bodies.

Some Ancestor Beings had a wider currency than one particular Aboriginal group. Several groups in Victoria, for example, have stories about an Ancestor Being called Bunjil. He is sometimes, as a result of this wide acceptance, called an All Father Being by scholars.

Dreaming stories

Aborigines had an oral rather than written tradition before the arrival of the white settlers. They handed on their wisdom from the Dreaming in the form of story, song and ritual. The Dreaming stories came from the Dreaming itself and record the sacred events of the Dreaming. They tell of the travels and the activities of the Ancestor Beings. The stories form a vast repertoire and each Aboriginal group has its own collection. Some stories were told to children, explaining, for example, why the emu does not fly. Children were often told only part of more complex, longer stories. As time went on the older children would be told more and the initiated adults told the full story with many layers of meaning. Some stories belonged only to women, some only to men.

At one level the Dreaming stories would tell of the Ancestor Beings and the events of the Dreaming. At another level they might give instruction on the natural environment, describing the characteristics of the flora and fauna, identifying sacred sites and giving practical rules for finding food and hunting. At yet another level they would give rules for living. We will return to this aspect when we deal more specifically with the ethics of Aboriginal religion.

The land in Aboriginal religion

There is obviously a very close link between the land and the Aboriginal groups. The land was and remains sacred. It is marked with sacred sites which are associated with the Ancestor Beings and which are identified in the Dreaming stories. These sacred sites are often linked up into Dreaming Trails which can cover hundreds of kilometres. Dreaming trails may be associated with a particular group or with an individual, and since Dreaming trails may overlap from one group to another they form a means of communication that includes commerce, marriage exchange and the sharing of religious ritual.

Particular groups of Aborigines are able to trace their lineage back to particular Ancestor Beings in a particular locale. Sacred objects, passed on carefully from one generation to another, validate their claim to the land associated with that Ancestor Being. Aborigines in this way become the guardians of the land.

The Ancestor Beings belonged to the Dreaming, the era of creation, but they are still present in the land. Aborigines have close links with them. The Ancestor Beings have a link with various animal, bird and plant species; a link with the environment which reflects their travels and activities or with a place that actually contains the transformed spiritual shape of the Ancestor Being. Aborigines are themselves linked with the presence of these Ancestor Beings. This link is called My Dreaming.

When scholars first described this link (which they did in a rather imperfect fashion) they made use of a term taken from North American Indian religion—totem. The Aborigines did not use the term. They used My Dreaming. Each Aborigine has a personal bond with the Ancestor Beings and with the Dreaming by means of My Dreaming or totem. The spiritual forces of the Ancestor Beings can enter into a woman's body and effect conception. For Aborigines this is more important than the human process of conception. The foetus and subsequent human child are directly linked with that Ancestor Being. The woman is able to identify where she was when conception occurred and which was the Ancestor Being to whom the conception should be attributed. This conception totem is not the only possible link. Sometimes groups are linked with Ancestor Beings, sometimes sex groups are linked. A particular Aborigine may be linked in various ways with various Ancestor Beings.

Ancestor Beings, land and the Aborigines are inextricably bound together. The land is sacred because of its connection with the Dreaming. It is not owned by the Aborigines. It is not to be treated with proprietorial airs. It is to be treated as a living companion. Sacred sites are not to be entered for any purpose except for religious usage. When white people appropriated land and made use of it for economic advantage then the Aboriginal religion was affronted and defiled. The land is a visible link between the Aborigines and their spirit world. It is a living reminder, a real presence, of what the Ancestor Beings did and continue to do.

Sacred ritual

The Aborigines need to maintain contact with the Dreaming. When they do so on a communal level they perform sacred rituals or ceremonies. It is in the performance of ritual that the Aborigines assert their own group solidarity, all being united with the Dreaming, and their personal identity with the Ancestor Beings. As the group celebrates it expresses joy, gratitude, and sometimes sympathy for others.

Some rituals are rites of passage. They occur at significant and critical moments in human life such as birth, attaining adulthood, marriage and death. A male initiation ceremony signifies the passage of a young man from boyhood to adulthood. The boy is first detached from his environment, where he had ready access to the women, and placed in isolation. There he receives instruction in the

Dreaming stories, is shown the sacred objects, taught the songs and ceremonies. He undergoes the initiation ceremony which often entails a symbolic death represented by circumcision or the removal of a tooth. He is then ready to assume his place among the initiated adults as a full member of the group with all its responsibilities.

Other rituals relate to the life of the group. Increase ceremonies assure the Aboriginal group that the food and other requisites they require will continue to be available. They do not ask for abundance or for more than they need; they live in harmony with their environment. Each group will be responsible for a particular food type and the sacred sites associated with that food. The spirit of each species is present in the sacred sites and the group is responsible for the ritual associated with them. Unless all species are maintained then the entire people will suffer. Everyone shares this responsibility.

Ritual is not exclusively a male domain. In the Roper River area women assemble for their own ritual. They make use of sacred song, dance and gesture and they celebrate the travels of the Munga Munga, female Ancestor Beings who were pioneers of that area. The Munga Munga had changed the landscape and their travels had brought a profound female presence into the land. The women, in their sacred song and dance, retrace the travels of the Munga Munga. They are responsible for maintaining this link with the Dreaming. Men are excluded from this ceremony.

As we consider Aboriginal ritual we realise that their religion has no priests or ministers. The transmission of the sacred stories, the performance of rituals, the care of sacred objects, are the responsibility of the whole group, even if the older men bear a greater share of that responsibility. Each individual is expected to learn the stories, hand them on, perform the rituals, identify and protect the sacred sites.

The role of women

The first anthropologists to describe Aboriginal religion were males. They were not given access to the women's realm, so they reported, mistakenly, that women were excluded from the sacred ritual. They thought that religion was the domain of men while the everyday life of gathering food, cooking and cleaning was the domain of Aboriginal women. More recently, particularly since more women have entered anthropology, it has become clear that women do perform an important role in Aboriginal religion. They have their own rituals, their own Dreaming stories and songs. They also perform in many rituals with men. Often they have important parts to play in the initiation rituals of boys. While it may be true that there is no equivalence between men and women in Aboriginal society, each having their own duties and sphere of responsibility, it is not simply the case that women are subservient and certainly not the case that women are excluded from Aboriginal religion.

The ethics of Aboriginal religion

In Aboriginal religion rock paintings, sacred stories and ritual replace the sacred books, commandments and sermons of other religions. The ethical justification of Aboriginal ways of behaviour comes from their belief in the Dreaming and from the Dreaming stories. The Dreaming dictates how their lives are to be lived.

The Dreaming, as transmitted in the Dreaming stories, established the structure of Aboriginal society, the way they lived their lives. Dreaming stories told of the complex kin relationships between the Ancestor Beings; these are to be reflected in the relationships among the Aboriginal people, who could relate to others in certain ways, could marry certain people, according to the pattern laid down in the Dreaming stories. The Ancestor Beings had travelled, danced, sung, spoken, drawn symbols in certain ways and these actions set down the precedent for Aboriginal people to follow.

Rules for individual living were also laid down in the Dreaming stories. There is, for example, in one Aboriginal group, the story of a brother and sister who lived incestuously together. Their father, outraged at their behaviour, arranged an accident in which both would be killed. The story lays down the rule prohibiting incest and prescribes the penalty of death.

There is a version of another Dreaming story that tells of the emu, Kalaia, and her sister the wild turkey, Kipara. Each had a family of the same number of chicks but Kalaia was jealous of Kipara. So Kalaia hid all but two of her chicks in tall grass and returned to camp and explained that she had killed the rest so that the two survivors could grow large and healthy. Kipara forthwith did the same, but when she returned with her two sole chicks she found that she had been tricked and that Kalaia still had all her family.

Several days later Kipara, now filled with revenge, folded up her wings tightly against her body. She danced in front of Kalaia and said that she had cut off her wings and thereby looked more beautiful. She also claimed to walk with less effort. Kalaia the emu took a stone knife and out of vanity really did cut off her wings. Kipara at once mocked her and pointed out that now she would be the prey of humans and dogs.

The Dreaming story explains on one level the facts that the emu does not fly and that the wild turkey produces clutches of only two eggs. As an ethical source the Dreaming story also explains that lying is prohibited and that vanity and deception are not acceptable.

However, it is not a simple matter of the Dreaming stories laying down a code of morality. The Ancestor Beings, in the Dreaming stories, at times murder, steal, lie, seduce, and act violently. While the stories sometimes provide models of exemplary behaviour, at other times they provide an image of the bad aspects of life. The Dreaming shows life as it is in the real world and from that image the Aborigine must derive a code of behaviour. In other religions it may be possible to describe the code of behaviour. This can be done only very generally in Aboriginal religion. All Aborigines would accept that a web connects them to each other, humans to the land, humans and the land to the Ancestor Beings. Whatever promotes that relationship is good. Hence individuals are expected to share food, to show respect for the elders, to marry within the kinship limits, to perform rituals at the proper place and time, to punish wrongdoers. Any action that disturbs the web of relationships is wrong. To murder or to marry a person forbidden by kinship is not so much a sin against the Ancestor Beings but a disruption of the whole framework in which Aboriginal people find harmony and life in their environment.

Non-Aborigines may misunderstand or disagree with the ethical system of the Aborigines because they would condone, under certain circumstances, infanticide. They also enforce strict punishment, even death, on people who break what in other cultures are considered to be minor rules. But the Aboriginal ethic can only be judged within its own frame of reference. The Aborigines lived a life close to nature. They had learned to adapt themselves to the environment in a way that no human has bettered. They accepted infanticide when another mouth to feed would have thrown the whole group life into jeopardy. They punished a sexual fault when it put impossible pressure on the whole group structure.

Europeans misunderstood Aboriginal religion and perhaps still do. In fact the first white settlers, in their ignorance, doubted if the Aborigines even possessed a religion. We know today that indeed they did and do possess a sophisticated religion which is highly adapted to their way of life. For those who are more used to monotheistic religions it takes a feat of empathy to understand it. In the end their religion and its ethic can only be admired.

Conclusion

There is a widespread tendency today for people to say that all religions are essentially the same, that they are paths leading to the same goal. In the Introduction this was the third easily identifiable attitude towards religion. Religious ethics detail the specifically religious reasoning for particular moral behaviour. What we have seen in the course of this book is that there is a great deal of overlap in the religious moral behaviour prescribed by the various world religions. There would seem to be little value in trying to classify such moral behaviours, particularly as religions add a variety of qualifications: 'You shall not kill, except when...' or 'Love your neighbour, but your "neighbour", is...'. What our study has shown, however, is that several types of religious reasoning exist that justify and promote moral behaviour. We have identified these as sacred stories, sacred texts, sacred ritual, social structure, religious experience and religious belief. We have tried to identify these ethical arguments and tried to see how, in each particular religion, they constitute a religious ethical system. Now, finally, we want to draw six general but important conclusions, which will help your understanding of religious ethics.

1 *A religious ethic may be based on a profound awareness of God as the creator and lord to whom people are accountable.*

This ethic justifies the type of morality with which most people in the West are familiar. Western civilisation has been significantly shaped by the moral convictions and attitudes of Jewish and Christian religion with their stress on the lordship of God. Islamic culture also shares many insights regarding God and humankind that had their origin in the experiences of ancient Israel.

The religions of Middle Eastern origin have a common vocabulary. God is our lord and we are his servants. God reveals his law and we must obey. The law may be quite specific as it was in Israel, the Ten Commandments being the core of a considerable body of legislation attributed to God. It is specific in Islam because the injunctions in the Qur'an are not seen as the opinions of a man, Muhammad, but as revelations of the divine will. It is less specific in early Christianity. While the moral law of Israel is not rejected, an all-embracing principle, love, is regarded as the supreme norm.

The language of law and obedience in these religions gives rise to other concepts. We are not always obedient; the divine law is often rejected or we refuse to render what is our due. Words like sin, penitence and forgiveness therefore appear in descriptions of the moral life. People are aware of how easily the relationship between God and themselves, the lord and his servants, can be broken. The restoration of this relationship becomes a paramount concern in the Middle Eastern religions. People may do something about it by means of sacrifice and penance. Or they may place their trust in the mercy and forgiveness of God. The idea of a divine grace that wipes away the guilt of failure is especially strong in the writings of the early Christians. It is present, too, in Judaism and Islam.

One result of this perception of the grace of God, particularly in Christianity, is that the motivation for a renewed obedience may be gratitude for what God is and what God has done. Love of God becomes the inspiration for doing what God wants. In this type of moral experience the demands of God cease to be laws, external to us, and accountability ceases to be the joyless obedience of those under authority. Rather, the will of God becomes our delight because the love of God for us engenders an answering love in those who both acknowledge his lordship and trust in his grace.

2 *Morality may be the expression of an internal principle or cosmic truth.*

It is often debated whether Theravada Buddhism should be regarded as a religion because of the absence from the Four Noble Truths of any idea of a god or gods. Defined narrowly as belief in a supernatural being, the term religion is not applicable to early Buddhism. It can be said, however, that it has a religious dimension, because of the transcendent quality of the experience a person can realise and the status of the doctrine taught by Buddha. The doctrine, the source of Buddhist morality, is regarded as the absolute truth about human life. For Theravada Buddhism what a person should do arises from what *is*, from what is the truth. The doctrine is not just a collection of ideas circulating in the mind of Buddha; it is the eternal and cosmic truth which he discovered and expounded. Buddhist morality lacks the sort of sanctions found in the Middle Eastern religions. Its atmosphere is quite different. But it does have at its core, a belief in a cosmic truth and cosmic law. In a similar way the Aboriginal belief in the Dreaming has closer links with Buddhism than the religions of the Middle East. The Dreaming is the explanation of all that is, all that has been, all that will be, both in place and in time. The Dreaming is the Aborigines' justification for moral behaviour, the source of all ethical justification.

Confucius, likewise, taught that the virtues people should seek were in conformity with the will or Way of Heaven. Heaven, in the Chinese tradition, is very different from the heavens of Middle Eastern religions. God is not the personal God of Judaism or Christianity and he is not a law-giver in the mould of Allah in Islam. In Confucianism, however, we should live according to certain principles because they are right. They are also vested with the authority of a past age. They constitute the Way, the Way of a power or reality beyond and above us. A great deal of the morality associated with Hinduism is also linked with belief in a cosmic order. *Dharma* is sacred law and *sanatana dharma*, 'everlasting law', is one of the terms used for the whole complex of duties which a Hindu should fulfil. The Code of Manu, the most detailed of descriptions of *dharma*, is attributed to the first human, a means of indicating that what is prescribed has its source beyond society, in an eternal order.

3 *The main thrust of a religious ethic may be the maintenance, transformation and/or perfecting of society.*

All religions have social effects. They encourage in their adherents attitudes that affect the life of society. Some, however, are more concerned than others (initially at least) with the state of the world. The aim of Confucius was to reform the China of his time. The stress on *dharma* in Hinduism has preserved, to a remarkable degree, the structure of the ancient social order despite disturbances caused by the many invaders who came into India from outside.

Belief in the great events of the Dreaming affects profoundly the Aborigines' attitude to the world and their environment. The land is, for them, a living thing; it is alive with the symbols of the Dreaming, alive with ultimate reality. It must therefore be respected and never exploited.

Islam was from the very beginning both a religion and a community. It taught a submission to God that encompassed both the individual and society. The ideal of devout Muslims has always been the transformation of the world into a realm where God reigns and where his law is obeyed.

Judaism was also an essentially communal faith which

saw the world as under the kingship of God. The visible manifestation of that sovereignty, the kingdom, was the great hope that sustained the faithful in Israel. It was their responsibility to manifest the kingship of God in their national life.

In its early years Christianity did not foster an interest in the transformation of the world. Belief in Jesus Christ was the faith of a community, the church, and the way of Christ was to be seen in the life of his followers. Early Christianity did not encourage participation in social change. There was no Christian crusade against slavery and other evils in the Roman Empire. Undoubtedly the smallness of the church and the expectation of an early end of the world were the main reasons for this attitude. When Christianity, from the fourth century onwards, became the faith of most of the people of Europe, it developed a wide-ranging concern with all aspects of social life. At times the church tried to dictate to rulers in matters of state law.

4 *The primary purpose of the moral path, on the other hand, may be the attainment of an individual experience.*

Buddhism, in its Theravada form, is a body of teaching which has the practical purpose of releasing individuals from the clutches of desire and bringing them to nirvana. Its ethical system and meditative discipline promise a new existence to the individual aspirant. It is true that a person treads the path with others in the life of the monastic order but it is the path of an individual; the necessary effort is that of an individual, as is the reward at the end. In Mahayana Buddhism also there is a promise of future glory for the individual. The Hindu mystic walks 'the way of knowledge' alone, no longer a part of the society which he has renounced.

In religions with a strong corporate and social character, living a good life is nevertheless accompanied by promises or expectations of blessings for individual believers. The

Confucian 'gentleman' is sustained by an inner calm because he walks the Way of Heaven. Hindus who do their duty perform an act of good *karma* which will lead to a better rebirth. In Islam, submission to the will of Allah results in *salam*, or peace. The other Middle Eastern religions have also promised their followers a peace, founded on the forgiving grace of God, and Christianity in particular has at times promised people blessedness, not only in this life but in a life to come. Individual mysticism, the quest for a personal transforming awareness of the Divine, has flourished in Christianity, Judaism and Islam.

5 *Religions differ in their view of the resources upon which people can draw to achieve their goals.*

The contrast between the two main forms of Buddhism is a striking illustration of how people can approach a religious goal from widely differing positions. For Theravada it is our own efforts, our own self-disciplined meditation, that will give us what we seek. The Mahayana Buddhists have many saviours in whom they can trust. Confucianism placed its confidence in moral education and in our innate power to realise our ideals. Hinduism likewise assumed that we could do our duty if we wanted to although *bhakti* adds the inspiration that comes from the love of God.

The Middle Eastern religions have insisted that we have the capacity to hear and respond to the word of God. God addresses us—through the prophets, Christ or the Qur'an—and we are free to obey. Christianity, however, developed a doctrine of human perversity which held that our obedience was always partial and always marred by self-interest. Harnessed to this view of our moral inadequacy was a complementary doctrine of divine grace, of grace as power and grace as forgiveness. As in Mahayana Buddhism, so in the Christian tradition, we can find in God a power that enables us to obey as we should.

6 *Religions vary in their adaptability to social change.*

It is clear enough in the West that many moral questions no longer receive the almost unanimous and clear-cut answers that they received in the past. This is partly due to the decline in religious belief and the rise of non-religious philosophies of human behaviour. It is also due to the emergence of new situations. Scientific technology, for example, poses questions that did not exist in earlier ages.

A religion has to be flexible if it is to have any relevance to new circumstances and new problems. It is possible, of course, for a religious tradition to ignore social situations and to concentrate, as mysticism tends to do, on individual experience. Modernisation need hardly touch the Hindu way of knowledge or the Zen Buddhist's quest for *satori*, illumination. The determination of China's rulers to give the country a new character has meant that Confucianism (in fact, all religions) must be rejected as irrelevant to the country's needs and goals.

Islam still has considerable prestige in the countries where it has been the dominant faith, but flexibility is difficult because of the substantial body of specific laws that are regarded as revealed by God. Modernisation has caused erosion of this legal edifice. In many Muslim countries today, laws are being formulated which ignore or modify the traditional religious law. Where this happens, it weakens the old-style authority of Islam and its legal experts. Modernist movements in Islam present the Qur'an as a source not so much of clear-cut law but of principles that can be applied in a variety of circumstances. On the other hand, there have been attempts in the last decade or so in some countries, notably Iran and Pakistan, to restore the age-old authority of Muslim law.

Over the centuries most Christian churches have also developed attitudes and convictions in the realm of ethics that claim the force of divine law. New ethical challenges

201

force a re-thinking of much that has been received from the past. If God is the living God and if love is the supreme law, then, many Christians say, Christianity should be applicable to the problems of this and every age. Such a flexibility relates not only to social challenges but also to the ideals and values of the individual.

Recommended reading

Judaism

CARMODY, J., CARMODY, D., & COHN, R. *Exploring the Hebrew Bible*. Prentice Hall, Englewood Cliffs, 1988. (A good coverage of the biblical tests of Judaism.)

COHEN, A. *Everyman's Talmud,* Schocken Books, New York, 1975. (A popular selection of readings from the Talmud.)

GOLDBERG, D. & RAYNER, J. *The Jewish People: Its History and Religion*. Penguin & Viking Press, London & New York, 1987. (An up-to-date presentation of Jewish history.)

JOHNSON, P. *A History of the Jews*. Weidenfeld & Nicolson, London, 1987. (Thorough and accurate. More scholarly.)

NEUSNER, J. *The Way of Torah*. Duxbury, London, 1979. (An inside view of Judaism and its teachings.)

UNTERMAN, A. *Jews: Their Religious Beliefs and Practices*. Routledge & Kegan Paul, Boston, 1981. (Very good on Jewish practice and beliefs. Written by a Jew.)

TREPP, L. *Judaism: Development and Life*. 3rd edn, Wodsworth, London, 1981. (Widely known text on Jewish thought.)

Christianity

CARMODY, D., & CARMODY, J. *Christianity: An Introduction*. Wodsworth, Belmont, 1988. (Easy-to-read coverage of Christian life and thought.)

FREND, W., *The Rise of Christianity*, Fortress Press, Philadelphia, 1984. (More technical coverage of the history of early Christianity.)

McBRIEN, R. P. *Catholicism*. 2 vols, Dove Communications, Melbourne, 1980. (The theology of Roman Catholicism without too much jargon.)

WALKER, W. et al. *A History of the Christian Church*. 4th edn, Charles Scribner's Sons, New York, 1985. (Standard, thorough history of the Christian Church.)

Islam

Al FARUQI, I. & Al FARUQI, I. *The Cultural Atlas of Islam*. Macmillan, New York, 1986. (Demonstrates the spread of Islam graphically.)

NASR, S. *Ideals and Realities of Islam*. 2nd edn, Allen & Unwin, Sydney, 1975. (Standard text on Islamic thought. More for the specialist.)

RAHMAN, F. *Major Themes of the Qur'an*. University of Chicago Press, Chicago, 1980. (Fairly technical but can be used in conjunction with the Qur'an.)

RUTHVEN, M. *Islam in the World*. 2nd edn, Longman, Melbourne, 1979. (Excellent presentation of Islam in the world of today.)

WATT, W. MONTGOMERY *What is Islam?* 2nd edn, Longman, Melbourne, 1979. (Classic on Islam written in an engaging manner.)

Hinduism

O'FLAHERTY, W. (tr.). *Hindu Myths*, Penguin Classics, Harmondsworth, 1975. (Contains many myths drawn from various sections of Hindu literature dealing with the actions of gods and demons.)

RAMANIJAN, A. K. (tr.). *Speaking of Siva*. Penguin Classics, Harmondsworth, 1973. (A collection of *bhakti* hymns from South India, the object of the devotion being the god Siva.)

SEN, R. C. *Hinduism*. Penguin Books, various edns. (Deals with the main features of Hinduism and gives extracts from some of the Hindu scriptures.)

SMART, N. *The World's Religions*. Cambridge University Press, London, 1989. (Standard cover of world religions by a leading scholar.)

Buddhism

CARRITHERS, M. *The Buddha*. Oxford University Press, Belmont, 1982. (Deals competently with history and thought of Buddhism.)

CONZE, E. (tr.). *Buddhist Scriptures*. Penguin Classics, Harmondsworth, 1975. (Contains selections from both Theravada and Mahayana scriptures.)

HUMPHREYS, C. *Buddhism*. Penguin, various edns. (Well-known classic written by British convert to Buddhism.)

SMART, N. *The World's Religions*. Cambridge University Press, London, 1989.

SWEARER, D. *Buddhism*. Argus Communications, Illinois, 1977. (Easy-to-read general introduction to Buddhism.)

Confucianism

LAU, D. C. (tr.). *Lao Tzu: Tao Te Ching*. Penguin Classics, Harmondsworth, 1963. (Good compendium of Chinese texts.)

SMART, N. *The World's Religions*. Cambridge University Press, London, 1989.

Australian Aboriginal culture and religion

BELL, D. *Daughters of the Dreaming*. Allen & Unwin, Melbourne, 1983. (Completes the missing female aspect of Australian Aboriginal religion.)

CHARLESWORTH, M. et al. *Religion and Aboriginal Australia: An Anthology*. University of Queensland Press, Brisbane, 1984. (Excellent collection of leading scholars on aspects of Australian Aboriginal religion.)

EDUCATION DEPARTMENT OF SOUTH AUSTRALIA. *An Introduction to Aboriginal Religion: Teachers' Handbook.* South Australian Government Printer, Adelaide, 1988. (Brief but succinct and accurate. Checked by Aborigines.)

EDWARDS, W. *An Introduction to Aboriginal Societies.* Social Science Press, Wentworth Falls, 1988. (Very readable introduction to Australian Aboriginal culture and history by a scholar who knows their life at first hand.)

Glossary

Admonition to Singala
This is a discourse on lay morality attributed to the Buddha. It is from the Digha Nikaya.

Apocalyptic
Literally an 'unveiling'. The term refers to a particular type of thinking and writing that began around 200 BCE and lasted until around 100 CE. It deeply affected early Christianity. Secret knowledge about the events surrounding the end of the world and the future was said to be 'unveiled' and revealed to certain initiates.

Chador
A traditional Iranian garment that covers a woman from head to foot.

Code of Manu
According to Hindu mythology, Manu is the progenitor of the human race. The Code, attributed to him, consists of rules governing the life of the individual and of society.

Digha Nikaya is from the second 'basket' or section of Theravada Scriptures. The threefold canon of Theravada is known as the *Tripitika* or 'Three baskets'.

Halachah
Jewish teaching that deals with ritual and moral behaviour, derived from the Talmud and later decisions of the Rabbis.

Hijra
Literally 'emigration'. The term refers to the journey of Muhammad from Mecca to Medina in 622 CE to establish the first Islamic community there. The Hijra established the Islamic calendar.

Instructions of Akshayamati
This is from a Mahayana collection of writings that dates from the seventh century. Earlier material is incorporated in it.

Ka'aba
The central shrine in the sacred city of Mecca. It is built in the shape of a cube, and predated Muhammad. It contains the Black Stone, believed by Muslims to be a fragment of the temple of Abraham. The Ka'aba is the focus of all Islamic prayer and of the hajj, the ritual pilgrimage to Mecca.

Mahabharata and Ramayana
These are the two epics of Hinduism. The former dates from the third or second century BCE, and the Gita is regarded as a later interpolation. The Ramayana is the story of Rama, who, like Krishna, is one of the *avataras*, or descents, of the god Vishnu. The vicissitudes of Rama and his wife Sita are known to all Hindus. Devotion to Rama is fostered by this account.

Mitzvah
A commandment, a religiously prescribed action, a good deed.

Pope
Literally 'father'. Normally the title Pope has been used of the Bishop of Rome whose authority is said to descend from Jesus through the apostle Peter. Roman authority over spiritual matters such as Church teaching and the regulation of morality developed at an early date. By the Middle Ages certain Popes claimed wide secular power as well.

Reformation
A widespread movement that attempted to bring about reform of the teaching and moral practice of the Western Christian Church in the sixteenth and seventeenth centuries. With regard to teaching, the Reformation claimed that it was recovering the original biblical heritage of early Christianity. The religious changes brought about by the

Reformation were accompanied by profound social and political upheavals that would divide Western Christianity between the Roman Catholic Church and the Protestants.

Sheol

A Jewish term designating the great cavern under the earth where all the dead would go regardless of the merit of their lives. Life in Sheol was not attractive. In the immediate pre-Christian phase of Judaism there was a widely held belief that God would resurrect the just from Sheol at the end of the world.

Shinto

Reference is made to the Japanese religious tradition of Shinto or Shintoism. This term means 'the way of the gods' and embraces the myths, beliefs, rituals and attitudes associated with *kami*, the 'superior beings' in Japanese history. Not all *kami* are fully developed gods. The word is also applied, for example, to places in nature that evoke awe, to royalty and to the spirits of ancestors. The most notable *kami* was the sun goddess who, according to Shinto mythology, was the ancestor of the first emperor. Shinto has at times fostered an intense loyalty to the Emperor and fervent Japanese patriotism.

Sutta Nipata

This is a poem in praise of the Buddhist virtues, especially *metta*. It comes from the second 'basket'.

Talmud

Literally 'learning'. This contains interpretations and elaborations of the Mishnah, the earliest code of Jewish oral law, which was arranged by Judah ha-Nasi at the beginning of the third century CE. The Talmud was completed about the fifth century CE.

Taoism

Taoism is referred to as one of the elements in Chinese religion. Its origins are associated with the teaching of Lao-tzu in the Tao Te Ching, 'The Way and its Power'. Opinions differ regarding the historicity of Lao-tzu and the date of this book. The traditional date is the sixth century BCE. The tao or Way in this particular writing is an impersonal cosmic principle underlying all things. The wise person seeks to live in conformity with this eternal tao. Taoism as a religion embraced the polytheism and spirit-worship of the majority of the population. It was viewed with scorn by Confucians.

Torah

Literally a 'teaching'. The term can be applied in a narrow sense to the first five books of the Bible, or it can be applied more broadly to the whole of Jewish teaching passed on from antiquity.

Umma

The technical religious term to describe the community of Islamic believers.

Upanishads

They come from the period following the Vedas. A large number of books are sometimes included but usually thirteen Upanishads are given a special status and regarded as normative.

Veda

'Knowledge'; this term is used for the earliest extant literature of Hinduism. There are four Vedas of which the Rig Veda, containing hymns used in the sacrificial ritual, is the best known. The Vedas were composed before 1000 BCE.

Index

abortion
   Jewish attitudes 39–40
   Christian attitudes 79–80
   Islamic attitudes 106
Allah 85, 91–7
Ancestor Beings 187–92
Arahat ('saint') 137
AUSTRALIAN ABORIGINAL RELIGIONS 181–93, 198
Australian Aboriginal ritual 188–90

Ba'al 17, 22
Beatitudes (in Gospel of Matthew) 56
Bhagavad Gita 123–7
bhakti ('devotion') 122–7, 129
Bodhisattva 149–50
Brahman 115
Buddha (Gautama) 133–5, 140, 148–50
BUDDHISM 131–55

Canaanites 16–17
caste (varna, jati) 118–20
CHRISTIANITY 45–81, 199
chun–tzu (Confucian 'gentleman') 167, 171–4
CONFUCIANISM 157–79, 197–8
Confucius (Kung Fu–tzu) 162–8
contraception
   Christian attitude 79–80
   Islamic attitude 106–7

covenant 18–20, 50
Covenant Code 23–25
culture and ethics 6–7

derek ('way') 20–1, 23
dharma ('duty' or 'teaching')
   in Hinduism 120–2, 124–6, 130, 198
   in Buddhism 135, 137

divorce
   Jewish attitude 29
   Christian attitude 55–6, 65–6
   Islamic attitude 106
Dreaming 185–8, 190
Dreaming stories 186, 187, 190–1

'emeth ('truth') 20, 23
'emunah ('faithfulness') 20, 23, 33
environmental ethics
   Jewish attitudes 39–40, 196
   Christian attitudes 74–76, 199
   Islamic attitudes 104
   Hindu attitudes 128
   Buddhist attitudes 152–3
   Confucian attitudes 177
   Australian Aboriginal attitudes 186–8, 198
ethics
   variety of 5–6
   language of 4
   religious 6–8
   sources of 9–10
euthanasia 81
Exodus 18–20

filial piety (Confucian) 170–1
Five Classics 163

Five Pillars of Islam 99–100
Five Relationships 168–70
Four Noble Truths 135–7, 138

Gospel of John 63–5
Gospel of Luke 61–2
Gospel of Mark 55–6
Gospel of Matthew 56–61
Greek Orthodoxy 66–7, 69–70

Halachah 33
ha'olam habbah ('the age–to–come') 48
ha'olam hazzeh ('this age') 48
hadith ('tradition') 97
hajj ('pilgrimage') 100
hesed ('covenant love') 20, 23, 25
HINDUISM 109–30
Hijra ('emigration') 90
history of Islam 85–92
history of Israel 15–20
holiness (in Judaism) 31–5
Holy Spirit 64–5

ijma ('consensus') 98
in vitro fertilisation 81
islam ('submission') 85, 99, 101
ISLAM 83–108, 201
Islamic resurgence 107

jen ('goodness') 171
Jesus 31, 50, 51–5, 112
Jewish festivals 37
jihad ('striving of holy war') 101
JUDAISM 13–44

ka'aba ('cube') 88, 92

karma
  in Hinduism 114–15
  in Buddhism 134–5, 146–7, 154

li ('appropriate behaviour') 175–6

Mahatma Gandhi 111–12
Mahayana Buddhism 133–4, 148–52, 199, 200
marriage
  in Judaism 29–30, 41
  in Christianity 79–80
  in Islam 105–6
medical ethics
  Jewish attitudes 40–1
  Christian attitudes 81
  Hindu attitudes 128
  Buddhist attitudes 153–4
  Chinese religious attitudes 178
medieval Judaism 36–7
Messiah 47–50
metta ('love') 144–5
mitzvah ('commandment') 33, 42
modern Judaism 36–38
moksa ('salvation') 118
morality
  characteristics of 4
Moses 18, 47
Muhammad 85–6, 88–92

Natural Law 72–3, 79–80
nirvana 137, 138, 141, 142
Noble Eightfold Path 136–7, 153

Orthodox Judaism 38

Paul of Tarsus 51–5

Pharisees 34–5
prophets of Israel 21–3
Protestant ethics 73–4

qiyas ('analogy') 98
Qumran 49
Qur'an 93–7, 196, 200, 201

Ramadan 99
Reform Judaism 38
Reformation 67–8
Roman Catholic Church 68
Roman Catholic Ethics 70–3

Sabbath 28, 37
samsara ('the cycle of life and death')
    in Hinduism 113, 116
    in Buddhism 134–5
sangha ('community of monks') 140, 141, 143–4, 154
sati 129
Sermon on the Mount 57–61
sexuality and ethics
    in Judaism 29–30
    in Christianity 79–81
    in Islam 105–6
shariah ('pathway') 93
Sheol 48
Shia Islam 100–2
Soka Gakkai 152
Sunnah ('custom') 97–8
Sufis 102–4
Sunni Islam 101

Ten Commandments 26–31
Ten Precepts 141–2, 144
Theravada Buddhism 133–4, 138, 197, 199

Torah 20–3, 31, 33–5, 50–1
Tripitika ('three baskets') 134
Triratna ('three jewels') 140, 144

umma ('community') 90
uncleanness in Judaism 36–7
Upanishads 113

Vatican Council II 72

Western Christianity 66
women and religious ethics
    in Judaism 41–3
    in Christianity 76–9
    in Islam 105–7
    in Hinduism 128–9
    in Buddhism 154–5
    in Chinese religions 178–9
    in Australian Aboriginal religions 190

Yahweh 15, 47, 50–2